Paleo
SLOW COOKER
COOKBOOK

Paleo
SLOW COOKER
COOKBOOK

EMILY DIONNE
MS, RD, LDN, CSSD, ACSM-HFS

FALL RIVER PRESS

New York

FALL RIVER PRESS

New York

An Imprint of Sterling Publishing
387 Park Avenue South
New York, NY 10016

FALL RIVER PRESS and the distinctive Fall River Press logo are registered trademarks of Barnes & Noble, Inc.

© 2013 by F+W Media, Inc.

Design by Gavin Motnyk

ISBN 978-1-4351-6154-2

For information about custom editions, special sales, and premium and corporate purchases, please contact Sterling Special Sales at 800-805-5489 or specialsales@sterlingpublishing.com.

Manufactured in China

2 4 6 8 10 9 7 5 3 1

www.sterlingpublishing.com

Contents

This book is dedicated to Brian.
Thank you for so many very special memories
that I will cherish forever, and for reminding us
all that life is far too short. I love you.

Acknowledgments

I would like to thank all of my clients, family, friends, and coworkers who provided their inspiration and support, all of which is represented in this book by the hundreds of delicious recipes—none of which could have been created without their help. A special thank-you to my clients at MBX Training, for their specialized input into the performance nutrition recipes, tailored toward athletes like themselves. Another special thank-you to my parents, who graciously took care of Buddy on those many late nights spent slow cooking. I truly appreciate everyone's suggestions, insight, and patience.

Introduction

IT IS NO SECRET that the Paleolithic diet has been pegged as one of the most difficult diets to follow. Although many recipes call for just a few ingredients, the challenges revolve around the amount of planning ahead required to bring these recipes to fruition. Cue the slow cooker! Slow cooking introduces New Age cooking methods to Stone Age sustenance. It incorporates a diverse range of fresh produce, herbs, and spices in each and every scrumptious concoction, while encouraging creativity, patience, and an open mind. The cavemen of the Paleolithic era did not have the privilege of utilizing this modern-day appliance. However, they did have their own way of slow cooking, by the only source of heat that was available—fire.

Slow cooking helps simplify the entire recipe process, both the cooking as well as the preparation. Fortunately, for the fairly simplistic, three-food-group-limited Paleo diet, slow cookers add both versatility and flair. This book comprises an extensive array of delicious and nutritious Paleo cuisine, including breakfast, lunch, dinner, and dessert dishes, ethnic cuisine, kid-friendly entrées, appetizers, and much more. The sizes of slow cookers used in these recipes range from 2-quart to 6-quart, and cooking times vary from less than 1 hour to greater than 10 hours.

The increasing popularity of the Paleo diet has led to the need for guidance in making it easier to follow, more convenient, and more conducive to our fast-paced, modern-day lifestyle. The Paleo way, sometimes referred to as eating "clean," can lead to a number of favorable health benefits for people of all ages and backgrounds, and as a result of some of these benefits, can also lead to improved sports performance in athletes. The diet is loaded with antioxidants, vitamins, minerals, and heart-healthy fats, all of which provide anti-inflammatory benefits, which can decrease one's risk of developing chronic diseases, including diabetes, cancer, cardiovascular disease, and osteoporosis. Following the diet can improve disease markers in those already suffering, and speed an athlete's recovery from training and competition, therefore improving strength gains, and ultimately, enhancing performance. The Paleo diet is also rich in fiber, which aids in regulating and improving digestion as well as maintaining more consistent energy levels, a key factor for both competitive athletes and avid exercisers. Some research also supports that this diet can improve an individual's weight management, overall body composition (i.e., decreased body fat percentage), and result in improvements in one's ability to control appetite.

There are some important modifications to the Paleo diet necessary to meet the specialized performance needs of athletes. Therefore, many of the recipes incorporate some "non-Paleo" foods such as starchy vegetables, sports drinks, and other liquid carbohydrates, in order to meet these needs. Two hours prior to competition, during competition, and up until ninety minutes following competition, specific non-Paleo foods should be consumed in order to prevent hindrance to performance, and to promote optimal recovery. Calcium and vitamin D supplements are sometimes recommended, depending on whether the athlete is willing to consume dairy and the amount of sunlight exposure he or she typically obtains. Consulting with a health care provider, team physician, or sports dietitian is important for athletes who follow the Paleolithic diet, especially for those just beginning the diet.

The hundreds of recipes included in the chapters to follow provide a diverse taste of the native cuisine of our primal ancestors, all slow-cooked for your enjoyment. Remember, there are no rules when it comes to the types and amounts of fresh herbs, spices, fruits, and vegetables you consume, so be creative, have fun, cook slow, and be well.

Chapter 1

Slow Cooking Nutritious and Delicious Cuisine for the Paleolithic Palate

The Paleolithic diet encompasses all principles of health and wellness. Adapting this lifestyle can help improve one's overall body composition, by both decreasing fat mass and increasing lean body mass. Some of the many potential health benefits of adopting a Paleolithic lifestyle include: improved health outcomes, decreased risk of disease, improved energy levels, and improved fitness levels and athletic performance. A major barrier to maintaining healthy behavior changes in today's society is time. Slow cooking is the perfect solution. With the use of a slow cooker, adopting a Paleolithic lifestyle can be simple and enjoyable.

The Paleolithic Era

Who would have thought that eating like a caveman would be a good idea? Little did we know how much knowledge our Paleolithic ancestors possessed. Even though they had to find, hunt, and kill most of their food, they were still making better choices than most in the world today. In addition, the exercise they endured while hunting their food was the icing on the cake. The Paleolithic humans had it right, while today's diets often include foods that are wreaking havoc on the human body.

Before the Neolithic time period, when development of agriculture and the domestication of animals became commonplace, Paleolithic humans were forced to survive off the land. They hunted wild game for protein and gathered fruits, vegetables, nuts, and seeds. There were no grains harvested, legumes cooked, or milk consumed past weaning. Our primal ancestors ate what they could find and they spent their lives hunting and gathering it. As a result, they were not exposed to many of the unhealthy additives present in some of our foods today.

Hunter-Gatherers

There are still some hunter-gatherers in existence today. They are peoples sustaining themselves and their families off of the land just as our ancestors of the Pleistocene epoch. Today, some examples of traditional hunter-gatherers that continue this lifestyle are the Bushmen of southern Africa, the Pygmies of central Africa, and the Spinifex people of western Australia. These tribes are practically free of the common ailments and killers of our generation today: heart disease, diabetes, arthritis, and cancer. Over time, issues with tooth decay, shorter life spans, infant mortality, and nutrient deficiencies were recorded more often. These are not issues that hunter-gatherers frequently faced.

Why is it that today's hunter-gatherers tend to be healthier than people in the rest of the world? From the outside, their lives appear to be much more difficult. They do not utilize modern medicine, modern shelter, or modern conveniences. They have no refrigeration to keep food for long periods of time. Yet, they survive and live healthier lives than most. Their genes are not constructed differently from the rest of the population, and they are certainly not a "super species" of humans. The secret lies within their diet.

Today's Paleolithic Diet

Now you may be thinking that you need to move to the forest and take up hunting, fishing, and gathering to comply with today's Paleolithic diet. That could not be further from the truth. The Paleolithic lifestyle simply requires a shift in your thinking. First, you need to learn what foods are considered Paleo "yes" or Paleo "no." Next, an initial shopping list, an open mind, and a whole bunch of recipes will start you on the journey toward Paleolithic success. Transitioning to a Paleo style of eating does not have to be an arduous task. In fact, many of the recipes adored by families all over the world can be converted quite simply to Paleo recipes with a few careful ingredient choices and some fun substitutions. For example, pasta is a staple in many households, but it is not included in the Paleolithic diet. A fantastic alternative to pasta is spaghetti squash. This amazingly delicious member of the squash family softens when cooked in the oven for less than 45 minutes, and with the light touch of a fork, its flesh can be pulled to form "strings" that resemble spaghetti.

Paleolithic hunter-gatherers ate foods that were preagricultural. They did not farm the land or herd animals for sustenance. Grains such as wheat, oats, barley, quinoa, and rice were not a part of their diet. White potatoes and legumes, such as soybeans and peanuts, also were not included.

How to Be Successful on the Paleolithic Diet Plan

As with any lifestyle change, you are sure to face obstacles along the way. What will you be able to eat when you're out with your friends? What are you going to prepare for each meal every day? How will you survive without soda and popcorn at the movies? This plan is not easy to initiate, but there are some ways to help ease the transition. These few tips and tricks will make this plan seem more manageable, more comfortable, and simply more fun.

Storage and Cooking in Bulk

An important component of ensuring your success is planning ahead. It is critical that you shop and cook in large amounts and store meals in containers for the future. Otherwise, you will be cooking around the clock and feel overwhelmed. An effective strategy would be to develop a routine where you cook three or four meals at one time and store them in the refrigerator or freezer.

Slow Cookers

Typically, you can find slow cookers where you find most small appliances. These mini ovens enable you to pack the most flavor into your food and give even the most inexperienced cooks confidence in the kitchen. They are simple to operate and practically foolproof, and best of all, you can throw everything in there and leave it to cook for hours at a time. Over the course of several hours your food will absorb the flavorings of spices and vegetables that you didn't know existed. This little invention creates a tasteful finished recipe that will leave you feeling like an accomplished chef.

Advantages to Slow Cooking the Stone Age Diet

Slow cooking is safe, easy, tasty, and even fun! Slow cooking is a slow process, and therefore, the time spent devoted to it is more appreciated, versus meals that require minimal time and preparation. It serves as the perfect way to counteract the hustle and bustle of today's society. It can help promote a *slower*, not-so-fast-paced lifestyle. The longer it takes to cook, the longer it should take to consume.

Slow cookers are extremely versatile. A slow cooker can accommodate a wide variety of dishes including soups and stews, main entrées, breakfast and brunch, meats, seafood, desserts, and even beverages. The Paleolithic diet is fairly restrictive, so incorporating the use of a slow cooker can help keep recipes new, fresh, and exciting.

Incorporating the use of slow cookers into the Paleo lifestyle helps increase acceptance and adherence. Ironically, it introduces some of the advantages of modern-day conveniences to an ancient, prehistoric way of life. Adding some of the benefits of today's fast-paced society through use of a slow cooker proves that quick and easy meal preparation can yield very healthy meals, and at the same time, it illustrates that a lifestyle based on ancient beliefs and practices can actually be very convenient. In a sense, slow cooking helps reverse some of the negative impacts of the modern-day, fast-paced lifestyle. It also serves as a reminder that the longer it takes for a meal to cook, the longer it should take to eat. Out with the fast. In with the slow.

Fifty percent of the ancient diet of the Paleolithic era was composed of fruits and vegetables, compared to a mere 10–15 percent of the modern diet. Ironically, all the fresh produce you desire is just miles away at the nearest grocery store. Our Stone Age ancestors handpicked their own.

A Menu the Whole Family Can Enjoy

The simplicity and safety of slow cooking allows for people of all ages to participate. Kid-friendly meals are very easily prepared. Therefore, encouraging kids to be involved in meal preparation teaches healthy cooking early on and decreases interest in other high-calorie, less nutritious foods. Teaching kids to cook at an early age improves the variety and nutrient density of their preferred food choices. It encourages autonomy and responsibility, while simultaneously instilling lifelong healthy behaviors.

More frequent visits to the grocery store are a huge part of adhering to the lifestyle. This shouldn't be viewed as a chore, however, but as a healthy experience that reinforces a new, healthier lifestyle with each visit! Engaging children in this experience is yet another positive step toward instilling *permanent* healthy habits.

There are a number of other potential health benefits kids can obtain from going Paleo. Traditional Paleo fare is free of many of the most common modern-day allergens, i.e., peanuts, milk, gluten, and soy. Avoiding allergens in popular and convenience foods can be extremely challenging for an adult, never mind for a child. Paleolithic-inspired foods also help promote healthy brain development, as they are rich in important micro- and macronutrients such as the omega-3 fatty acids eicosapentaenoic acid (EPA) and docosahexaenoic acid (DHA), and antioxidants like vitamins E, C, and A, which help protect the body against free radical damage.

Incorporating "kid-friendly" meals and encouraging every child's participation in meal preparation are positive steps toward preventing childhood obesity. Slow cooking healthy, nutritious meals leaves kids feeling energized and focused rather than sluggish and overly full from modern-day fast, convenient, processed foods. Kids who are more in tune with healthy eating are more health conscious, and are able to witness first hand the positive impact of good nutrition on their health and performance in sports and in the classroom.

Primal Food for Prevention and Health Promotion

Probably the most significant benefit of adhering to a Paleolithic lifestyle is the potential for decreasing one's risk of developing a number of chronic diseases such as cancer, diabetes, cardiovascular disease, osteoporosis, and so on. Of course, you can decrease your risk of developing diseases by way of a well-balanced, nutrient-dense modern-day diet, low in unhealthy fats, processed foods, refined carbohydrates, and preservatives. However, the popularity of Paleolithic nutrition continues to expand, and people of all ages, demographics, and fitness levels are climbing aboard and sailing back to ancient ways, perhaps in an attempt to reverse and/or avoid the negative impact that years of unhealthy eating habits and sedentary lifestyles have caused.

Heart Healthy

The high fiber, low saturated fat, and high antioxidant and micronutrient content of the Paleo diet has many heart-healthy benefits. Such a diet composition can result in improved cholesterol profiles, decreased cardiac risk scores, and improved blood pressure status. It can promote a healthier heart and an overall healthier future.

Cancer Fighting

The Paleo diet provides a number of disease-fighting, cancer-preventing components. Its high dietary fiber content, coupled with an abundance of vitamins, minerals, and antioxidants, as well as the strict avoidance of processed trans fats and refined, processed sugars, together create a strong line of defense against numerous types of cancer.

Optimization of Overall Health and Wellness

Adherence to a Paleolithic lifestyle can also help in the prevention and management of chronic diseases like obesity (defined by a Body Mass Index, or BMI, above 30), diabetes, and osteoporosis. It encourages a naturopathic-based, organic, and purer perception as well as a greater ownership of one's health and well-being. Self-awareness and establishing a more health-conscious perception of oneself are important steps along the road to becoming and staying well.

Body mass index (BMI), which is calculated using an individual's weight (in kilograms) divided by his or her height (in meters, squared), is used to classify whether someone is of normal weight, overweight, or in the obesity range. A BMI of 25–29.9 is considered overweight, and obesity is classified by a BMI greater than or equal to 30.

Prehistoric Metabolism

It is more than just what the cavemen put in their mouths that allowed them to maintain healthier weight profiles and a better overall body composition than their modern-day counterparts. Resting metabolism (your metabolic rate) naturally declines with age. This is due to the decrease in one's muscle mass over time, which in turn is due to the decline in physical activity over time. Paleolithic times did *not* promote or even allow for any sort of sedentary lifestyle. To survive, one had to move, hunt, gather, keep moving, and so on, thus preserving muscle mass for a longer period during adulthood.

It is pretty difficult to gain weight on a diet composed predominantly of fruits and vegetables! However, animal protein is a large component of the Paleo diet, and excess saturated fats and calories can easily be consumed without careful consideration of food choices and meal preparation.

Longevity Without Medicine

Health and metabolism may have been more easily maintained in pre-historic times, despite the fact that advances in modern medicine were not available for them to take advantage of. If the two worlds collided—prehistoric lifestyle meets modern medicine—it could very well be the best of both worlds. Hence, the ever-growing popularity of Paleolithic nutrition.

Fuel for Fitness

Avid exercisers and competitive athletes are becoming increasingly inter-ested in adopting a Paleolithic-themed lifestyle. As many engage in exercise to relieve stress and enhance overall health and wellness, their preference for a pure, fresh, less processed, and more organic diet frequently ensues. Retracing the footsteps of our Paleolithic ancestors is an easy task for some, more challenging for others, yet tempting to many. It is important to set clear fitness and performance goals—and to ensure proper nutrition—in order to not only complement, but optimize these goals. When consistently and appropriately adhered to, the Paleolithic diet plan can play a key role in the pursuit of maximum performance.

Competitive athletes and others involved in periods of intense training and competition have more complex nutrient requirements. The work of Loren Cordain, PhD, a professor and well-known researcher in Paleolithic nutrition, laid the groundwork for the special considerations developed for athletes who follow the Paleolithic diet. Cordain's *The Paleo Diet for Athletes* recommends that athletes increase their consumption of essential carbohydrates to meet their specialized performance needs, and it provides nutrient timing guidelines for doing so. The recommendations for implementing necessary variations to the Paleo diet are influenced by an increased need for carbohydrates before, during, and after training and competition. Non-Paleo starches and sugars are encouraged during these times, in order to adequately prefuel, maintain, and refuel. Adequate carbohydrates, fluids, and electrolytes are critical for preventing injury and enhancing recovery.

Awaken the Senses

The naturopathic-themed approach of the Paleo lifestyle to health and well-being promotes an overall wakening of the senses. The variety of fresh herbs and spices helps enhance enjoyment of eating. Adopting mindful eating practices creates more openness to and acceptance of new foods, promoting a greater appreciation and understanding of where our foods actually come from. Slow cooking is a perfect way to illustrate the joy of mindful eating. It gives the experience of seeing and smelling and thus savoring the food, even hours before sitting down to eat.

Slow cooking allows for more variety and diversity, with the ability to use numerous fresh herbs, spices, and natural seasonings. Variety is crucial to preventing boredom, and thus maximizes adherence to a desired lifestyle; therefore, slow cooking Paleolithic dishes makes the lifestyle easier to stick with!

Processed Foods Out, Natural Fare In

Slow cooking, especially that of Paleolithic fare, prohibits the use of processed, packaged food products. Eating clean, in a sense, is enjoying cuisine free of additives, chemicals, and toxins, while embellishing wholesome, true ingredients. It serves as a twofold approach to health: Paleolithic nutrition helps eliminate the potentially negative impacts of the modern-day diet by simply avoiding the center of the supermarket, while enhancing overall nutritional intake by shopping solely along the perimeter.

Modernizing the Paleolithic Lifestyle

The conveniences of modern-day society place the world at our fingertips. Cavemen, with no access to any kind of technology or other conveniences of our modern-day lifestyle, survived and thrived on a Paleolithic lifestyle. Therefore, there is no reason it can't be done today. As technology and other modern advancements have evolved, there has been a corresponding decline in the significance placed on healthy eating and exercise. A lack of time is typically the most common excuse used for both. Isn't the purpose of technology to help make life easier, and better? Instead of allowing modern-day stressors to serve as a permanent excuse for not achieving a healthy lifestyle, why not take advantage of these modern tools? Simplify. Slow cook!

Chapter 2

Rise and Shine: Slow-Cooking Breakfasts

Breakfast Burrito Filling

Wrap cooked ingredients in pan-fried egg whites formed to a size similar to a tortilla, and serve with your favorite breakfast burrito toppings.

INGREDIENTS | SERVES 4

1¼ pounds lean boneless pork, cubed

12 ounces diced tomatoes with green chilies

1 small onion, diced

1 jalapeño, diced

½ teaspoon ground chipotle

¼ teaspoon cayenne pepper

¼ teaspoon ground jalapeño pepper

2 cloves garlic, minced

Place all the ingredients into a 2-quart slow cooker. Stir. Cook on low for 8 hours. Stir before serving.

PER SERVING: Calories: 188 | Fat: 5g | Protein: 32g | Sodium: 70mg | Fiber: 0.5g | Carbohydrates: 2g | Sugar: 1g

"Hard-Boiled" Eggs

This old-fashioned, hard-boiled breakfast staple has never been so simply prepared.

INGREDIENTS | SERVES 12

12 large eggs

1. Place 12 eggs in a 6-quart slow cooker. Cook on high for 2 hours.

2. Gently remove eggs and place in bowl of ice water (which loosens the shell for peeling). Peel, and enjoy!

PER SERVING: Calories: 72 | Fat: 5g | Protein: 6g | Sodium: 70mg | Fiber: 0g | Carbohydrates: 0.5g | Sugar: 0g

Slow-Cooked Scrambler

Preparing a warm and hearty scrambled egg dish is a breeze in the slow cooker.
A delicious start to the day.

INGREDIENTS | SERVES 2

1 tablespoon canola oil, plus more for greasing slow cooker

6 eggs

6 tablespoons coconut milk

Freshly ground black pepper, to taste

Seasonings of choice, to taste

1 cup chopped vegetables of choice: e.g., mushrooms, onions, peppers

1 teaspoon minced garlic

1 teaspoon mustard

1. Turn a 4-quart slow cooker on low and add canola oil. Grease the sides of the slow cooker with additional oil, as needed.

2. In a medium bowl, whisk together the eggs and coconut milk and season with pepper to taste. Add any other seasonings to the eggs and whisk the ingredients together.

3. Add 1 cup chopped vegetables of your choosing to the bowl, along with 1 teaspoon of minced garlic and 1 teaspoon of mustard, and mix.

4. Transfer the egg mixture to the slow cooker, cover, and cook on low for 1 hour.

5. Stir the eggs with a fork to help break them up to cook evenly. Cook the scrambled eggs, covered, for 1 more hour. Stir the eggs again with a fork.

PER SERVING: Calories: 362 | Fat: 31g | Protein: 20g | Sodium: 245mg | Fiber: 0.5g | Carbohydrates: 3g | Sugar: 1g

Breakfast Casserole

Cook this overnight and you're guaranteed to impress this season's holiday house guests!

INGREDIENTS | SERVES 4

1 pound lean ground beef (85% lean or higher)

1 small onion, diced

1 teaspoon freshly ground black pepper

1 teaspoon garlic powder

1 teaspoon red pepper flakes

12 eggs

1 cup coconut milk

Canola oil for greasing slow cooker (about 1 tablespoon)

1 small butternut squash, peeled, seeded, and sliced

1. In a skillet over medium heat, start to cook the ground beef. Add the onion and spices, cooking just until the onion is soft, about 8–10 minutes (you don't need to finish cooking the beef—it will finish in the slow cooker).

2. In a large bowl, whip together the eggs and coconut milk.

3. Grease the inside of a 4- to 6-quart slow cooker. Add the squash, the beef/onion mixture, and then the egg/milk mixture. Stir and make sure that all of the food is covered by the egg/milk mixture. Cook on low for 8–10 hours. Slice and serve warm.

PER SERVING: Calories: 491 | Fat: 33g | Protein: 44g | Sodium: 293mg | Fiber: 1g | Carbohydrates: 5.5g | Sugar: 2g

Cinnamon Stewed Plums

Serve as a breakfast fruit, or as a dessert with a whipped topping.

INGREDIENTS | SERVES 4

½ cup honey

1 cup water

Dash salt

1 tablespoon fresh lemon juice

1 cinnamon stick

1 pound fresh ripe plums (about 8 small or 6 medium), pitted

1. Combine all ingredients in a 2- to 4-quart slow cooker and cook on low for about 6 hours, or until plums are tender.

2. Serve warm, chilled, or at room temperature.

PER SERVING: Calories: 181 | Fat: 0g | Protein: 1g | Sodium: 43mg | Fiber: 2g | Carbohydrates: 48g | Sugar: 46g

Ground Chicken and Carrot Quiche

This high-protein recipe can be served for breakfast, lunch, or dinner.

INGREDIENTS | SERVES 2

6 large eggs
½ pound ground chicken, browned
1 cup shredded carrots
½ cup beef broth
5 tablespoons coconut milk
4 tablespoons fresh minced parsley
½ teaspoon coriander
Coconut oil for greasing slow cooker

1. In a medium bowl, beat eggs well with a wire whisk.

2. Add the chicken, carrots, and all remaining ingredients except coconut oil, and stir.

3. Grease the bottom and sides of a 2- to 4-quart slow cooker with coconut oil. Add the egg mixture to slow cooker, cover, and cook on low for 1 hour.

4. Stir the eggs with a fork to help break them up for even cooking. Cover, and cook on low for 1 hour. Fluff with a fork and serve warm.

PER SERVING: Calories: 551 | Fat: 40g | Protein: 40g | Sodium: 538mg | Fiber: 2g | Carbohydrates: 8g | Sugar: 4g

Slow-Cooked Eggs Florentine

*This egg recipe can be prepared using a variety of vegetables.
Feel free to experiment with tomatoes, artichokes, zucchini, etc.*

INGREDIENTS | SERVES 3

Cooking spray or coconut oil for
greasing slow cooker

1 (10-ounce) package frozen, chopped
spinach, thawed and drained

1 (8-ounce) can mushrooms, drained

¼ cup chopped onion

6 large eggs, beaten

1 cup coconut milk

1 teaspoon freshly ground black pepper

½ teaspoon dried oregano

½ teaspoon dried basil

½ teaspoon garlic powder

1. Spray a 4- to 6-quart slow cooker with nonstick cooking spray or grease with coconut oil.

2. Layer the spinach, mushrooms, and onions on bottom of slow cooker.

3. In a medium bowl, combine the eggs, coconut milk, pepper, and all other seasonings, and pour mixture into slow cooker.

4. Cover and cook on high for 1½–2 hours or until center is hot. Spoon out onto individual plates, and serve warm.

PER SERVING: Calories: 341 | Fat: 27g | Protein: 18g |
Sodium: 542mg | Fiber: 4g | Carbohydrates: 12g | Sugar: 3g

Southwestern Breakfast Bake

*Perfect for brunch, or a special-occasion late breakfast with family or friends,
as this dish takes a minimum of 4 hours to cook.*

INGREDIENTS | SERVES 8

8 large eggs
1 (7-ounce) can of green chilies, drained
2 cups coconut milk
1 cup sliced mushrooms
1 red bell pepper, seeded and diced
1 small onion, diced
1 cup diced tomatoes
¾ teaspoon lemon juice
½ teaspoon freshly ground black pepper
2 (10-ounce) packages frozen spinach,
   thawed, undrained

1. Combine all ingredients except spinach in a bowl and whisk together.

2. Layer ⅓ of the spinach (about 3 ounces) on bottom of 4-quart slow cooker. Pour ½ of egg mixture on top of spinach. Put another layer of spinach (about 3 ounces) on top of egg mixture, and top with remaining egg mixture. Top with the remaining spinach. Cover and cook on low for 6–7 hours or on high for 4–5 hours.

3. Uncover a few minutes before serving, and cook on high to allow finished product to dry out.

PER SERVING: Calories: 227 | Fat: 18g | Protein: 11g |
Sodium: 134mg | Fiber: 3g | Carbohydrates: 10g | Sugar: 4g

Paleo-Approved Zucchini Nut Bread

Top this sweet bread with some Apple Butter (page 36), Peach Marmalade (page 33), or other fruit spread found later in this chapter.

INGREDIENTS | SERVES 8

3 eggs, beaten

½ cup sunflower oil

½ cup unsweetened applesauce (or Awesome Applesauce, page 72)

1 teaspoon orange extract

¼ cup honey

2 teaspoons baking soda

1 teaspoon baking powder

1 teaspoon ground cinnamon

1 cup hazelnuts, ground to the consistency of coarse meal

1 cup pecans, ground to the consistency of coarse meal

1 cup almond powder

1 cup chopped walnut pieces

¾ pound zucchini, grated

Nonstick cooking spray

1. Preheat a round 5-quart slow cooker, covered, on high for 15 minutes.

2. Blend together the first eight ingredients in a large bowl. Stir in the nuts and zucchini.

3. Spray the bottom and lower sides of the preheated slow cooker with the cooking spray.

4. Pour the batter evenly into the slow cooker. Cover and bake for 45–60 minutes, or until sides of the bread pull away from sides of slow cooker and the tip of a knife inserted into the center, held to the count of five, comes out clean.

PER SERVING: Calories: 238 | Fat: 17g | Protein: 8g | Sodium: 406mg | Fiber: 3g | Carbohydrates: 17g | Sugar: 12g

Rubble Porridge

This Stone Age–inspired hot cereal is loaded with fiber, vitamin E, and omega-3 fatty acids.

INGREDIENTS | SERVES 6

½ cup raisins and cranberries

¼ cup slivered almonds

¼ cup raw pumpkin seeds

¼ cup raw sunflower seeds

¼ cup unsweetened coconut

⅛ cup honey

2 tablespoons coconut butter, melted

1. Place all dry ingredients in a 4-quart slow cooker, add honey and butter, and toss well.

2. Cover (but vent with a chopstick) and cook on high for 2½–3½ hours, stirring periodically to prevent burning.

3. Cool porridge. Enjoy with almond or coconut milk.

PER SERVING: Calories: 160 | Fat: 9g | Protein: 4g | Sodium: 3mg | Fiber: 2g | Carbohydrates: 19g | Sugar: 14g

Apples Supreme

Enjoy the treasures of apple-picking season with this melt-in-your-mouth dish, another recipe that can be served as a breakfast fruit or warm dessert.

INGREDIENTS | SERVES 8

4 Granny Smith apples, peeled, cored, and sliced

4 Golden Delicious apples, peeled, cored, and sliced

¾ cup honey

½ teaspoon ground cinnamon

½ teaspoon ground cloves

½ cup coconut butter

Place apples in a 4-quart slow cooker and toss with remaining ingredients. Cover and cook on low for 4–5 hours. Serve warm.

PER SERVING: Calories: 97 | Fat: 0g | Protein: 0g | Sodium: 2mg | Fiber: 1g | Carbohydrates: 26g | Sugar: 26g

Blackberry Jam

This easy low-sugar jam does not need to be canned; it will keep up to a month in the refrigerator.

INGREDIENTS | YIELDS 1 QUART

3 cups fresh blackberries
1¾ ounces no-sugar pectin
½ cup honey
¾ cup water

1. Place all the ingredients in a 2-quart slow cooker. Stir.

2. Cook on high, uncovered, for 5 hours. Using a fork or potato masher, smash the berries a bit until they are the texture you prefer. Pour jam into an airtight container.

3. Refrigerate overnight before using.

PER SERVING: Calories: 701 | Fat: 2g | Protein: 7g | Sodium: 16mg | Fiber: 23g | Carbohydrates: 181g | Sugar: 160g

Pear Clafouti

Clafouti is a soft pancake-like breakfast with fruit. If you choose to use a larger slow cooker than the specified 2½-quart size, you will need to reduce the cooking time. When the sides are golden brown and a toothpick stuck in the middle comes out clean, the clafouti is done.

INGREDIENTS | SERVES 4

2 pears, stems and seeds removed, cut into chunks, and peeled if preferred
½ cup almond flour
½ cup arrowroot starch
2 teaspoons baking powder
½ teaspoon xanthan gum
⅓ cup honey
1 teaspoon ground cinnamon
2 tablespoons coconut butter, melted
2 eggs
¾ cup (full-fat) coconut milk
1 tablespoon vanilla extract

1. Place pears in a greased 2½-quart slow cooker.

2. In a large bowl, whisk together the almond flour, arrowroot starch, baking powder, xanthan gum, honey, and cinnamon.

3. Make a well in the center of the dry ingredients and add melted coconut butter, eggs, coconut milk, and vanilla. Stir to combine wet with dry ingredients.

4. Pour batter over pears. Cover slow cooker and vent lid with a chopstick or the handle of a wooden spoon.

5. Cook on high for 2½–3 hours or on low for 5–6 hours. Serve warm or cold with a slow-cooked Paleo fruit sauce, like Cran-Apple (page 70) or Summer Berry (page 62).

PER SERVING: Calories: 404 | Fat: 19g | Protein: 7g | Sodium: 291mg | Fiber: 5g | Carbohydrates: 56g | Sugar: 32g

Peach Marmalade

You can spread this on a Paleo fruit dish, or try it on Paleo-Approved
Zucchini Nut Bread (page 30).

INGREDIENTS | YIELDS 8 CUPS

2 pounds peaches, peeled, pitted, and chopped

½ cup (about 6 ounces) dried apricots, chopped

1 (20-ounce) can pineapple tidbits in unsweetened juice, undrained

2 medium oranges

1 small lemon

2 cups honey

2 (3-inch) cinnamon sticks

Innovative Peach Marmalade Uses

By keeping this marmalade the consistency of applesauce, you have the added versatility of using it as a condiment to top cooked chicken breasts—mix it with a Paleo barbecue or chili sauce to create a sweet and savory dipping sauce. Or, simply use it to replace applesauce in many different recipes.

1. Add peaches to a food processor or blender along with the apricots and pineapple (with juice).

2. Grate the orange and lemon peels and add zest to the food processor or blender. Cut the oranges and the lemon into quarters and remove any seeds, then add to the food processor or blender. Pulse until entire fruit mixture is pulverized. Pour into a greased 4- to 6-quart slow cooker.

3. Add the honey to the slow cooker and stir to combine with the fruit mixture. Add the cinnamon sticks. Cover and cook on low for 4 hours, stirring occasionally, until the mixture reaches the consistency of applesauce. When finished cooking, remove the cinnamon sticks.

4. Unless you process and seal the marmalade into sterilized jars, store in covered glass jars in the refrigerator for up to 3–4 weeks. The marmalade can also be frozen for up to 6 months.

PER SERVING: (1 cup) | Calories: 352 | Fat: 0g | Protein: 2g | Sodium: 5mg | Fiber: 3g | Carbohydrates: 94g | Sugar: 90g

Chai Tea

Store any leftover tea in a covered container in the refrigerator.
It can be reheated, but leftover tea is best served over ice.

INGREDIENTS | SERVES 12

5 cups water
6 slices fresh ginger
1 teaspoon whole cloves
2 (3-inch) cinnamon sticks
1½ teaspoons freshly ground nutmeg
½ teaspoon ground cardamom
1 cup honey
12 tea bags
6 cups coconut milk

Sweet Tip

If you prefer, skip the honey during the cooking process and serve it alongside the tea instead. Each drinker can add the honey to his or her serving according to taste.

1. Add the water to a 4-quart slow cooker. Put the ginger and cloves in a muslin spice bag or a piece of cheesecloth that has been rinsed, wrung dry, and secured with a piece of kitchen twine; add to the cooker along with the cinnamon, nutmeg, and cardamom. Cover and cook on low for 4–6 hours or on high for 2–3 hours.

2. Stir in the honey until it's dissolved into the water. Add the tea bags and coconut milk; cover and cook on low for ½ hour. Remove and discard the spices in the muslin bag or cheesecloth, the cinnamon sticks, and the tea bags. Ladle into tea cups or mugs to serve.

PER SERVING: Calories: 312 | Fat: 24g | Protein: 2g | Sodium: 19mg | Fiber: 0g | Carbohydrates: 27g | Sugar: 23g

Autumn-Inspired, Vanilla-Flavored Poached Fruits

Enjoy as breakfast or as dessert. Follow a Paleo dish with this concoction as a sweet end to a hearty meal.

INGREDIENTS | SERVES 5

2 Granny Smith apples, peeled, cored, and halved (save cores)

2 Bartlett pears, peeled, cored, and halved (save cores)

1 orange, peeled and halved

⅔ cup honey

1 vanilla bean, split and seeded (save seeds)

1 cinnamon stick

1. Place apple and pear cores in a 4½-quart slow cooker.

2. Squeeze juice from orange halves into slow cooker and add the orange halves, honey, vanilla bean and seeds, and cinnamon.

3. Add apples and pears, and pour in enough water to cover the fruit. Stir, cover, and cook on high for 2–3 hours, until fruit is tender.

4. Remove apple and pear halves and set aside. Strain cooking liquids into a large saucepan and simmer gently over low heat until the liquid reduces by half and thickens. Discard apple and pear cores.

5. Dice apples and pears and add to saucepan to warm.

6. To serve, spoon fruit with sauce into bowls.

PER SERVING: Calories: 150 | Fat: 0g | Protein: 0g | Sodium: 2mg | Fiber: 1g | Carbohydrates: 40g | Sugar: 40g

Apple Butter

Depending on when you start this recipe, it can take up to two days to complete. It is great for giving an "autumn-like" feel to just about any side dish, main entrée, dessert, or even a hot or iced beverage.

INGREDIENTS | YIELDS 5 CUPS

6 apples, peeled, cored, and quartered
½ tablespoon vanilla extract
⅔ cup honey
1 teaspoon ground cinnamon
¼ teaspoon ground cloves

1. Place apples and vanilla extract in a 4- to 6-quart slow cooker. Cover and cook on low for 8 hours.

2. Mash apples with a fork. Stir in honey, cinnamon, and cloves.

3. Cover and cook on low for 6 hours. Allow to cool at room temperature or in the refrigerator for 1–2 hours. Serve chilled or at room temperature.

PER SERVING: (1 cup) | Calories: 235 | Fat: 0g | Protein: 1g | Sodium: 2mg | Fiber: 3g | Carbohydrates: 62g | Sugar: 57g

Strawberry Jelly

Almond butter and strawberry jelly make the perfect pair—"AB & J" (Almond Butter and Jelly, page 206).

INGREDIENTS | SERVES 24

1½ quarts red, ripe strawberries, hulled

3¾ cups honey

¼ cup lemon juice

1. Place the strawberries in a 4-quart slow cooker. Stir in the honey and lemon juice. Cover and cook on high for 2½ hours, stirring twice.

2. Uncover and continue cooking 2 hours longer, or until preserves have thickened, stirring occasionally.

3. Ladle into hot, sterilized half-pint jelly jars, seal, and store in the refrigerator for up to 2 weeks.

PER SERVING: (3 ounces) | Calories: 173 | Fat: 0g | Protein: 0g | Sodium: 3mg | Fiber: 1g | Carbohydrates: 47g | Sugar: 45g

Pear Butter

Enjoy pear season all year long! Drizzle over some fresh fruit salad for a sweet addition to a traditional breakfast favorite.

INGREDIENTS | SERVES 8

8 pears of any variety, peeled, cored, and sliced

2 cups water

¾ cup honey

Juice of 1 lemon

1 whole star anise

¼ teaspoon ginger

¼ teaspoon nutmeg

1. Place all ingredients in a 6-quart slow cooker, cover, and cook on low for 10–12 hours.

2. Uncover and cook on low for an additional 10–12 hours, until thick and most of the liquid has been absorbed.

3. Allow to cool and remove the star anise, then purée in a blender. Store in airtight canning jars.

PER SERVING: (4 ounces) | Calories: 196 | Fat: 0g | Protein: 1g | Sodium: 5mg | Fiber: 5g | Carbohydrates: 53g | Sugar: 43g

Apricot Butter

Makes a tasteful substitute for orange marmalade.

INGREDIENTS | SERVES 8

5 ripe apricots, peeled, pitted, and puréed

1½ cups honey

2 teaspoons ground cinnamon

1 teaspoon ground cloves

1½ tablespoons lemon juice

1. Pour puréed apricots into a 4- to 6-quart slow cooker and add honey, spices, and lemon juice. Mix well.

2. Cover and cook on high for 8–10 hours, removing cover halfway through cooking. Stir periodically.

3. Store in the refrigerator in an airtight canning jar, or freeze.

PER SERVING: (4 ounces) | Calories: 413 | Fat: 0g | Protein: 1g | Sodium: 8mg | Fiber: 2g | Carbohydrates: 11g | Sugar: 109g

Blueberry Butter Bliss

A blueberry lover's dream. This antioxidant-rich spread proves blueberries really are a superfood!

INGREDIENTS | SERVES 7

4 cups fresh blueberries, puréed

¾ cup honey

Zest of ½ lemon

1 teaspoon cinnamon

¼ teaspoon grated nutmeg

1. Pour puréed blueberries into a 4- to 6-quart slow cooker and cover. Cook on low for 5 hours.

2. Remove lid and add the honey, lemon zest, and spices, mixing well. Turn heat up to high, and cook for another hour, uncovered.

3. Once butter is cooked down sufficiently, pour into canning jars and cover tightly.

4. Process canning jars in boiling water for 10 minutes. Store unopened jars in a cool, dark place.

PER SERVING: (4 ounces) | Calories: 161 | Fat: 0g | Protein: 1g | Sodium: 2mg | Fiber: 2g | Carbohydrates: 43g | Sugar: 38g

Blackberry and Apple Preserves

A not-so-traditional combination of two widely enjoyed, versatile fruits.

INGREDIENTS | SERVES 13

2 pounds cooking apples, peeled, cored, and chopped
3 cups honey
1¾ cups blackberries
2 tablespoons lemon juice
1 lemon rind, grated

1. Place all the ingredients in a 4- to 6-quart slow cooker, cover, and cook on high for 4–5 hours, stirring periodically.

2. Pour jam into warmed canning jars and allow to cool.

3. Cover and store in refrigerator for up to 2 months.

PER SERVING: (4 ounces) | Calories: 280 | Fat: 0g | Protein: 1g | Sodium: 4mg | Fiber: 2g | Carbohydrates: 75g | Sugar: 72g

Fig Jam

A versatile spread sure to liven up any Paleo breakfast sweet bread or fruit dish, and loaded with fiber and phytonutrients.

INGREDIENTS | SERVES 3 (½-CUP SERVINGS)

2 pounds fresh figs, peeled, cut into eighths
1 cup honey
½ cup water
1 lemon, diced, including the rind, seeds removed
3 tablespoons finely diced crystallized ginger

1. Add all the ingredients to a 2- to 3-quart slow cooker. Cover and cook on high for 4 hours.

2. Remove cover and cook an additional 1–2 hours, until mixture reaches a jam-like consistency.

3. While still hot, pour into clean, sterilized 4-ounce jars, and store covered in the refrigerator for up to 3 weeks.

PER SERVING: (½ cup) | Calories: 570 | Fat: 1g | Protein: 3g | Sodium: 9mg | Fiber: 9g | Carbohydrates: 152g | Sugar: 142g

Chapter 3

Appetizers

Hot and Spicy Nuts

Serve these at a cocktail party as an alternative to plain salted nuts.
They are also delicious stirred into trail mix.

INGREDIENTS | YIELDS 2½ CUPS

2½ cups skin-on almonds or mixed nuts

1 teaspoon canola oil

½ teaspoon ground jalapeño pepper

½ teaspoon powdered garlic

½ teaspoon cayenne pepper

½ teaspoon ground chipotle chile
  pepper

½ teaspoon paprika

1. Place the nuts into a 2- to 4-quart slow cooker. Drizzle with the oil. Stir. Add the spices, and then stir again to distribute the seasonings evenly.

2. Cover and cook on low for 1 hour. Then uncover and cook on low for 15 minutes or until the nuts look dry.

PER SERVING: Calories: 1,417 | Fat: 122g | Protein: 51g | Sodium: 4mg | Fiber: 30g | Carbohydrates: 54g | Sugar: 9g

Slow-Cooked Salsa

This may be the easiest salsa recipe ever, but it tastes so much fresher than jarred salsa.

INGREDIENTS | SERVES 10

4 cups grape tomatoes, halved

1 small onion, thinly sliced

2 jalapeño peppers, diced

⅛ teaspoon salt

1. Place all ingredients into a 2-quart slow cooker. Stir. Cook on low for 5 hours.

2. Stir and lightly smash the tomatoes before serving, if desired.

PER SERVING: Calories: 4 | Fat: 0g | Protein: 0g | Sodium: 0.5mg | Fiber: 1g | Carbohydrates: 1g | Sugar: 0.5g

Baba Ghanoush

This dish can be served as an appetizer, a side dish, a dip,
or even a salad. Serve this with fresh vegetables.

INGREDIENTS | SERVES 12

1 (1-pound) eggplant
2 tablespoons tahini
2 tablespoons lemon juice
2 cloves garlic

Tahini Tips

Tahini is a paste made from ground sesame seeds. The most common tahini uses seeds that have been toasted before they are ground, but "raw" tahini is also available. The two can be used interchangeably in most recipes, but occasionally a recipe will specify one or the other. Look for tahini near the peanut butter, in the health food section, or with the specialty foods in most grocery stores.

1. Pierce the eggplant with a fork. Cook on high in a 4-quart slow cooker for 2 hours.

2. Allow the eggplant to cool. Peel off the skin. Slice it in half and remove the seeds. Discard the skin and seeds.

3. Place the pulp in a food processor and add the remaining ingredients. Pulse until smooth.

PER SERVING: Calories: 25 | Fat: 1g | Protein: 1g | Sodium: 4mg | Fiber: 2g | Carbohydrates: 3g | Sugar: 1g

Pumpkin Bisque

This simple soup is a perfect first course at a holiday meal or an easy light lunch.

INGREDIENTS | SERVES 4

2 cups puréed pumpkin

4 cups water

1 cup unsweetened coconut or almond milk

¼ teaspoon ground nutmeg

2 cloves garlic, minced

1 large onion, minced

Make Your Own Pumpkin Purée

Preheat the oven to 350°F. Slice a pie pumpkin or an "eating" pumpkin into wedges and remove the seeds. Place the wedges on a baking sheet and bake until the flesh is soft, about 40 minutes. Scoop out the flesh and allow it to cool before puréeing it in a blender.

1. Place all ingredients into a 4-quart slow cooker. Stir. Cook on low for 8 hours.

2. Use an immersion blender to blend until smooth, or blend in batches in a standard blender. Serve hot.

PER SERVING: Calories: 85 | Fat: 7g | Protein: 1g | Sodium: 12mg | Fiber: 2g | Carbohydrates: 6g | Sugar: 2g

Beef Taco Filling, Paleo Style

Smoky hot chipotle peppers give this filling a rich spicy flavor. Try it wrapped in iceberg or romaine lettuce leaves and topped with shredded carrots, avocado, and tomato.

INGREDIENTS | SERVES 8

1½ pounds 94% lean ground beef

1 large onion, minced

15 ounces canned fire-roasted diced tomatoes

1 Anaheim pepper, minced

2 chipotle peppers in adobo, minced

½ teaspoon cumin

½ teaspoon cayenne pepper

½ teaspoon paprika

½ teaspoon garlic powder

½ teaspoon oregano

1. Sauté the beef and onion in a nonstick skillet for about 5–10 minutes, until just browned. Drain off any grease. Add to a 4-quart slow cooker. Break up any large pieces of beef with a spoon.

2. Add the remaining ingredients and stir. Cook on low for 7 hours. Stir prior to serving.

PER SERVING: Calories: 139 | Fat: 4g | Protein: 18g | Sodium: 56mg | Fiber: 0g | Carbohydrates: 2g | Sugar: 1g

Chicken Taco Filling, Paleo Style

Try different variations of this recipe using ground turkey or ground veal.

INGREDIENTS | SERVES 8

1½ pounds lean ground chicken

1 large onion, minced

1 (15 ounce) can fire-roasted diced tomatoes

1 Anaheim pepper, minced

2 chipotle peppers in adobo, minced

½ teaspoon cumin

½ teaspoon cayenne pepper

½ teaspoon paprika

½ teaspoon garlic powder

½ teaspoon oregano

1. Sauté the chicken and onion in a nonstick skillet for about 4–8 minutes, until just browned. Drain off any grease. Add to a 4-quart slow cooker. Break up any large pieces of chicken with a spoon.

2. Add the remaining ingredients and stir. Cook on low for 7 hours. Stir prior to serving.

PER SERVING: Calories: 185 | Fat: 13g | Protein: 15g | Sodium: 65mg | Fiber: 0g | Carbohydrates: 2g | Sugar: 1g

Enchilada Filling, Paleo Style

This recipe is an excellent way to use up leftover chicken or turkey, and it makes enough filling for two 9" × 13" pans of enchiladas (8 enchiladas, using large lettuce leaves, per pan). Make one pan and freeze the other for another time.

INGREDIENTS | SERVES 8

3 jalapeño peppers, halved

1 teaspoon canola oil

1 large onion, diced

3 cloves garlic, minced

1 teaspoon dried oregano

1 teaspoon cayenne pepper

½ teaspoon cumin

1 (28 ounce) can crushed tomatoes

¾ cup Chicken Stock (page 78)

1 tablespoon lime juice

4 cups shredded cooked chicken or turkey

1. Place the jalapeño peppers cut-side down on a broiler pan. Broil on low for 2 minutes or until they start to brown. Allow to cool, and then dice.

2. In a nonstick skillet, heat the oil over medium heat. Add the onion, garlic, and jalapeño peppers, and sauté until the onions are soft, about 5 minutes.

3. Add the onion mixture to a 4-quart slow cooker. Add the remaining spices, crushed tomatoes, stock, and lime juice. Cook on low for 5–6 hours, then add the shredded meat. Turn up to high and cook for an additional hour.

PER SERVING: Calories: 158 | Fat: 6g | Protein: 21g | Sodium: 93mg | Fiber: 1g | Carbohydrates: 4g | Sugar: 1g

Don't Overfill

Leave at least an inch of headroom in the slow cooker. The lid needs to fit tightly for the slow cooker to cook properly; otherwise the liquid ingredients may boil over, leaving you with a potentially dangerous situation and quite a mess.

Pork and Tomatillo Burrito Filling, Paleo Style

Serve this filling with tomatoes, lettuce, and avocado in large iceberg or romaine lettuce leaves.

INGREDIENTS | SERVES 2

½ pound boneless lean pork tenderloin roast
¾ cup diced tomatillos
¼ cup sliced onions
½ jalapeño pepper, diced
1 tablespoon lime juice

1. Place all ingredients into a 2-quart slow cooker. Stir. Cook on low for 8–10 hours.

2. Use a fork to shred all of the contents. Toss to distribute the ingredients evenly.

PER SERVING: Calories: 147 | Fat: 3g | Protein: 24g | Sodium: 61mg | Fiber: 1g | Carbohydrates: 5g | Sugar: 3g

Stuffed Grape Leaves

Although there are many versions of grape leaves served across the Mediterranean, these grape leaves are inspired by Greece.

INGREDIENTS | SERVES 30

16 ounces jarred grape leaves (about 60 leaves)

Cooking spray, as needed

¾ pound 94% lean ground beef, chicken, or pork

1 shallot, minced

¼ cup minced dill

½ cup lemon juice, divided

2 tablespoons minced parsley

1 tablespoon dried mint

1 tablespoon ground fennel

¼ teaspoon freshly ground black pepper

2 cups water

1. Prepare the grape leaves according to package instructions. Set aside.

2. Spray a nonstick skillet with cooking spray. Sauté the meat and shallot until the meat is thoroughly cooked. Drain off any excess fat. Scrape into a bowl and add the dill, ¼ cup lemon juice, parsley, mint, fennel, and pepper. Stir to incorporate all ingredients.

3. Place a leaf, stem-side up, on a clean work surface, with the top of the leaf pointing away from you. Place 1 teaspoon filling in the middle of the leaf. Fold the bottom toward the middle and then fold in the sides. Roll it toward the top to seal. Repeat until all leaves are used.

4. Place the rolled grape leaves in two or three layers in a 4-quart oval slow cooker. Pour in the water and remaining lemon juice. Cover and cook on low for 4–6 hours. Serve warm or cold.

PER SERVING: Calories: 21 | Fat: 1g | Protein: 3g | Sodium: 11mg | Fiber: 0g | Carbohydrates: 0g | Sugar: 0g

Slow-Cooked Almonds with a Kick

These crunchy, heart-healthy snacks are hard to resist.

INGREDIENTS | SERVES 24

6 cups whole, unblanched almonds

4 tablespoons coconut oil

3 cloves garlic, minced

2–3 teaspoons coarsely ground black pepper

1. Heat a 4-quart slow cooker on high for 15 minutes. Add the almonds.

2. Drizzle oil over almonds and stir. Sprinkle with garlic and pepper, and stir.

3. Cover and cook on low for 2 hours. Stir every 30 minutes.

4. Turn heat up to high, and cook uncovered for 30 minutes, stirring every 15 minutes.

5. Turn heat to low and serve warm, or remove from heat and allow to cool.

PER SERVING: Calories: 138 | Fat: 12g | Protein: 5g | Sodium: 0.5mg | Fiber: 3g | Carbohydrates: 5g | Sugar: 1g

Eggplant Relish

Serve with grilled or raw veggies for dipping.

INGREDIENTS | SERVES 6

1 large eggplant, pierced all over with fork

2 tablespoons extra-virgin olive oil

½ cup finely chopped tomato

¼ cup finely chopped onion

¼ cup almond yogurt

3 cloves garlic, minced

½ teaspoon dried oregano

1–2 tablespoons lemon juice

Freshly ground black pepper, to taste

1. Place pierced eggplant in a 4-quart slow cooker, cover, and cook on low until tender, 4–5 hours. Cool to room temperature.

2. Cut eggplant in half and remove eggplant pulp (including the seeds) from the peel with a spoon. Mash eggplant pulp and mix with olive oil, tomato, onion, almond yogurt, garlic, and oregano. Season with lemon juice and pepper and serve.

PER SERVING: Calories: 49 | Fat: 5g | Protein: 0g | Sodium: 2mg | Fiber: 0g | Carbohydrates: 2g | Sugar: 1g

Buffalo Chicken Wings

These spicy wings make the perfect tailgate treat.

INGREDIENTS | SERVES 12

4 tablespoons canola or coconut oil (or a combination of these)

4 tablespoons hot pepper sauce

1 tablespoon lime juice

Freshly ground black pepper, to taste

4 pounds chicken wings with wing tips removed, cut in half

Try 'em boneless!

For the boneless version of this classic appetizer, replace wings with 4 pounds of boneless, skinless tenders. Be prepared to eat with a fork! Serve as an appetizer as is, or on top a bed of salad greens.

1. Add oil, hot pepper sauce, and lime juice to a 4- to 6-quart slow cooker. Cook on high for about 15–20 minutes.

2. Add small amount of pepper to wings and broil in the oven until lightly browned, about 5–6 minutes on each side.

3. Add chicken wings to slow cooker, and stir to coat with the sauce. Cover and cook on high for 3–4 hours.

PER SERVING: Calories: 372 | Fat: 28g | Protein: 27g | Sodium: 233mg | Fiber: 0g | Carbohydrates: 0g | Sugar: 0g

Spiced Cashews

This fiery favorite can liven up any appetizer menu.

INGREDIENTS | SERVES 24

6 cups cashews

3 tablespoons olive or canola oil

3 tablespoons crushed dried rosemary

1 tablespoon honey

¾ teaspoon cayenne pepper

½ teaspoon garlic powder

1. Heat a 2- to 4-quart slow cooker on high for 15 minutes; add cashews. Drizzle oil over cashews and toss; add remaining ingredients and toss.

2. Cover and cook on low for 2 hours, stirring every hour. Turn heat to high, uncover, and cook 30 minutes, stirring after 15 minutes.

3. Turn heat to low to keep warm for serving or remove from slow cooker.

PER SERVING: Calories: 20 | Fat: 2g | Protein: 0g | Sodium: 0mg | Fiber: 0g | Carbohydrates: 1g | Sugar: 1g

Appetizer Meatballs

Combine the cooked meatballs in a slow cooker with a sauce from Chapter 4, like Jalapeño-Tomatillo Sauce (page 60) or Pink Tomato Sauce (page 64), to enhance the flavor of these versatile meatballs.

INGREDIENTS | YIELDS 24 MEATBALLS

1 pound lean ground beef
1 egg
2 tablespoons dried minced onion
1 teaspoon garlic powder
½ teaspoon freshly ground black pepper

1. Add all the ingredients to a large mixing bowl and combine with your clean hands. Shape the resulting mixture into approximately 24 meatballs.

2. Add meatballs to a 2- to 4-quart slow cooker, cover, and cook on high until meatballs are cooked through, about 4 hours.

3. Turn heat to low and keep warm before serving.

PER SERVING: (1 meatball) | Calories: 29 | Fat: 1g | Protein: 4g | Sodium: 15mg | Fiber: 0g | Carbohydrates: 0g | Sugar: 0g

Slow-Cooked Paleo Party Mix

Grab it while it's hot, because it won't last long once the guests arrive!

INGREDIENTS | SERVES 24

4 tablespoons canola oil
3 tablespoons lime juice
2 teaspoons garlic powder
2 teaspoons onion powder
1 cup raw almonds
1 cup raw pecans
1 cup raw walnut pieces
1 cup raw cashews
2 cups raw pumpkin seeds, shelled
1 cup raw sunflower seeds, shelled

1. Add canola oil to a 2-quart slow cooker. Then add the lime juice, garlic powder, and onion powder, and stir all together.

2. Next, add the nuts and seeds. Stir well until all are evenly coated. Cover and cook on low for 5–6 hours, stirring occasionally.

3. Uncover, stir, and cook another 45–60 minutes, to dry the nuts and seeds.

4. Cool and store in airtight container.

PER SERVING: Calories: 207 | Fat: 19g | Protein: 7g | Sodium: 2mg | Fiber: 3g | Carbohydrates: 5g | Sugar: 1g

Spinach Bake

Serve with vegetable dippers or Paleo-friendly crisps!

INGREDIENTS | SERVES 8

1 (10-ounce) package frozen spinach, thawed, undrained

1 small onion, finely chopped

1 stalk celery, thickly sliced

1 clove garlic

2 tablespoons olive oil

½ teaspoon dried basil

½ teaspoon dried thyme

⅛ teaspoon ground nutmeg

Freshly ground black pepper, to taste

2 eggs

1. In a food processor, process the spinach, onion, celery, garlic, oil, basil, thyme, and nutmeg until finely chopped.

2. Season to taste with pepper. Add eggs and process until smooth.

3. Spoon the mixture into a greased, 1-quart souffle dish, and place the dish inside a 6-quart slow cooker.

4. Cover and cook on low about 4 hours.

PER SERVING: Calories: 63 | Fat: 5g | Protein: 3g | Sodium: 48mg | Fiber: 1g | Carbohydrates: 3g | Sugar: 1g

Chicken Chowder

A warm, traditional taste of home. A great first course to a hearty poultry dish on a cold winter's night.

INGREDIENTS | SERVES 5

1 pound skinless, boneless chicken thighs (cut up into chunks)

1 (14½-ounce) can diced tomatoes

1 (8-ounce) package fresh, sliced mushrooms

1 large red onion, minced

4–6 cloves garlic, minced

½ cup Chicken Stock (page 78)

½ cup dry red wine

1 teaspoon dried oregano

1 teaspoon dried basil

1 teaspoon freshly ground black pepper

1. Place all ingredients into a 4-quart slow cooker.

2. Cover and cook on low for 6 hours, stirring occasionally.

PER SERVING: Calories: 162 | Fat: 4g | Protein: 19g | Sodium: 239mg | Fiber: 1g | Carbohydrates: 8g | Sugar: 2g

Bison Stew

Bison contains fewer calories, less fat, and more iron per serving than both beef and chicken!

INGREDIENTS | SERVES 4

2 small onions, sliced

6 whole large carrots, peeled and sliced

1 bell pepper, diced

3 stalks celery, diced

2 jalapeño peppers, diced

2 pounds bison meat, cut into 1-inch cubes

1 (28-ounce) can fire-roasted tomatoes

½ cup Jalapeño-Tomatillo Sauce (page 60)

Handful of fresh cilantro, chopped

1 tablespoon oregano

Freshly ground black pepper, to taste

1. Place onions, carrots, bell pepper, celery, and jalapeño peppers in bottom of a 4- to 6-quart slow cooker. Add bison meat and all remaining ingredients.

2. Cover and cook on low for 6–8 hours. Serve hot.

PER SERVING: Calories: 95 | Fat: 1.5g | Protein: 2g | Sodium: 103mg | Fiber: 6g | Carbohydrates: 20g | Sugar: 9g

Coconut Shrimp

An irresistibly sweet way to enjoy a popular appetizer.

INGREDIENTS | SERVES 6

3½ cups Chicken Stock (page 78)

1 cup water

1 teaspoon ground coriander

1 teaspoon ground cumin

Cayenne pepper, to taste

Zest of 1 lime

⅓ cup lime juice

7 cloves garlic, minced

1 tablespoon minced fresh ginger

1 large onion, chopped

1 red bell pepper, diced

1 whole large carrot, peeled and shredded

½ cup flaked coconut

½ cup golden raisins

1½ pounds large or jumbo shrimp, peeled and thawed if frozen

Toasted coconut, for garnish

1. Mix the chicken stock, water, coriander, cumin, cayenne pepper, lime zest, lime juice, garlic, and ginger in a 4- to 6-quart slow cooker.

2. Stir in the onion, bell pepper, carrot, flaked coconut, and raisins.

3. Cover and cook on low for 3 hours.

4. Stir in the shrimp. Cover and cook another 30 minutes.

5. Serve garnished with toasted coconut.

PER SERVING: Calories: 232 | Fat: 4g | Protein: 28g | Sodium: 380mg | Fiber: 2g | Carbohydrates: 21g | Sugar: 12g

Carrot Pudding

Serve this pudding chilled in the summer heat and enjoy warm in the cold winter season.

INGREDIENTS | SERVES 4

4 large carrots, cooked and grated

1 small onion, grated

¼ teaspoon nutmeg

1 tablespoon honey

1 cup coconut milk

3 eggs, beaten

½ teaspoon lemon juice

1. Mix together carrots, onion, nutmeg, honey, milk, eggs, and lemon juice.

2. Pour into a 2- to 4-quart slow cooker and cook on high for 3–4 hours.

PER SERVING: Calories: 218 | Fat: 16g | Protein: 7g | Sodium: 110mg | Fiber: 2g | Carbohydrates: 15g | Sugar: 9g

Hot Cinnamon-Chili Walnuts

These seasoned walnuts are a surprising hit with chili powder, cinnamon, and honey.

INGREDIENTS | SERVES 6

1½ cups walnuts

¼ cup honey

2 teaspoons cinnamon

1½ teaspoons chili powder

2 teaspoons coconut oil

1. Combine all the ingredients and place in a greased 2½-quart slow cooker.

2. Cover and vent the lid with a chopstick or the handle of a wooden spoon. Cook on high for 2 hours or on low for 4 hours. If using a larger slow cooker, you will probably need to reduce the cooking time to only 1 hour on high, or 2 hours on low.

3. Pour walnut mixture out onto a baking sheet lined with parchment paper. Allow to cool and dry and then transfer to a container with an airtight lid. Store in the pantry for up to 2 weeks.

PER SERVING: Calories: 238 | Fat: 19g | Protein: 5g | Sodium: 8mg | Fiber: 3g | Carbohydrates: 16g | Sugar: 12g

Roasted Pistachios

Raw pistachios are available at Trader Joe's (www.traderjoes.com) or health food stores. Roasting your own lets you avoid salt on the nuts, which makes them a snack that perfectly matches your Paleo palate.

INGREDIENTS | SERVES 16

1 pound raw pistachios
2 tablespoons extra-virgin olive oil

Putting Roasted Pistachios to Work

You can make 8 servings of a delicious coleslaw alternative by mixing together 3 very thinly sliced heads of fennel; ½ cup roasted, chopped pistachios; 3 tablespoons extra-virgin olive oil; 2 tablespoons freshly squeezed lemon juice; and 1 teaspoon finely grated lemon zest. Taste for seasoning and add freshly ground black pepper and additional lemon juice if desired. Serve immediately or cover and refrigerate up to 1 day.

1. Add the nuts and oil to a 2-quart slow cooker. Stir to combine. Cover and cook on low for 1 hour.

2. Stir the mixture again. Cover and cook for 2 more hours, stirring the mixture again after 1 hour. Store in an airtight container.

PER SERVING: Calories: 172 | Fat: 14g | Protein: 6g | Sodium: 0mg | Fiber: 3g | Carbohydrates: 8g | Sugar: 2g

Chapter 4

Sauces and Spreads

Jalapeño-Tomatillo Sauce

Serve this sauce over a fiery southwestern dish for a little more spice.

INGREDIENTS | SERVES 4

1 teaspoon canola oil
2 cloves garlic, minced
1 medium onion, sliced
7 large tomatillos, diced
2 jalapeño peppers, minced
½ cup water

1. Heat the oil in a nonstick pan over medium heat. Sauté the garlic, onion, tomatillos, and jalapeño peppers for 5–10 minutes, until softened.

2. Place the mixture into a 4-quart slow cooker. Add the water and stir. Cook on low for 8 hours.

PER SERVING: Calories: 14 | Fat: 1g | Protein: 0g | Sodium: 1mg | Fiber: 0g | Carbohydrates: 1g | Sugar: 0g

Fruity Balsamic Barbecue Sauce

Use this sauce in pulled pork, as a dipping sauce, over chicken or burgers, or even as a marinade.

INGREDIENTS | SERVES 20

¼ cup balsamic vinegar
2½ cups cubed mango
2 chipotle peppers in adobo, puréed
1 teaspoon honey

1. Place all ingredients into a 2-quart slow cooker. Stir. Cook on low for 6–8 hours.

2. Mash the sauce with a potato masher. Store in an airtight container for up to 2 weeks in the refrigerator.

PER SERVING: Calories: 19 | Fat: 0g | Protein: 0g | Sodium: 2mg | Fiber: 0g | Carbohydrates: 5g | Sugar: 4g

Lemon Dill Sauce

Serve this delicious, tangy sauce over salmon, asparagus, or chicken.

INGREDIENTS | SERVES 4

2 cups Chicken Stock (page 78)
½ cup lemon juice
½ cup chopped fresh dill
¼ teaspoon white pepper

Place all the ingredients into a 2- to 4-quart slow cooker. Cook on high, uncovered, for 3 hours or until the sauce reduces by one-third.

PER SERVING: Calories: 51 | Fat: 2g | Protein: 3g | Sodium: 179mg | Fiber: 0g | Carbohydrates: 6g | Sugar: 3g

A Peek at Peppercorns

Black peppercorns are the mature fruit of the black pepper plant, which grows in tropical areas. Green peppercorns are the immature fruit of the pepper plant. White peppercorns are mature black peppercorns with the black husks removed. Pink peppercorns are the dried berries of the Brazilian pepper.

Raspberry Coulis

A coulis is a thick sauce made from puréed fruits or vegetables. In this recipe, the slow cooking eliminates the need for puréeing because the fruit cooks down enough that straining is unnecessary. Delicious as both a breakfast fruit spread or sweet dessert topping.

INGREDIENTS | SERVES 8

12 ounces fresh or frozen raspberries
1 teaspoon lemon juice
2 tablespoons honey

Place all the ingredients into a 2-quart slow cooker. Mash gently with a potato masher. Cook on low for 4 hours uncovered. Stir before serving.

PER SERVING: Calories: 16 | Fat: 0g | Protein: 0g | Sodium: 0mg | Fiber: 0g | Carbohydrates: 4g | Sugar: 4g

Taste, Taste, Taste

When using fresh berries, it is important to taste them prior to sweetening. One batch of berries might be tart while the next might be very sweet. Reduce or eliminate honey if using very ripe, sweet berries.

Fennel and Caper Sauce

Try this sauce over boneless pork chops or boneless, skinless chicken breasts and grilled summer vegetables.

INGREDIENTS | SERVES 4

2 fennel bulbs with fronds, thinly sliced

2 tablespoons nonpareil capers

½ cup Chicken Stock (page 78)

2 shallots, thinly sliced

2 cups diced fresh tomatoes

½ teaspoon freshly ground black pepper

⅓ cup fresh minced parsley

1. Place the fennel, capers, stock, shallots, tomatoes, and pepper in an oval 4-quart slow cooker.

2. Cook on low for 2 hours, and then add the parsley. Cook on high for an additional 15–30 minutes.

PER SERVING: Calories: 64 | Fat: 1g | Protein: 3g | Sodium: 108mg | Fiber: 5g | Carbohydrates: 13g | Sugar: 3g

Summer Berry Sauce

Drizzle this sauce over desserts and breakfast foods.

INGREDIENTS | SERVES 20

1 cup raspberries

1 cup blackberries

1 cup golden raspberries

½ cup water

½ teaspoon honey

Place all the ingredients into a 2-quart slow cooker. Lightly mash the berries with the back of a spoon. Cover and cook on low for 2 hours, then uncover and turn on high for ½ hour.

PER SERVING: Calories: 10 | Fat: 0g | Protein: 0g | Sodium: 0mg | Fiber: 1g | Carbohydrates: 2g | Sugar: 1g

Artichoke Sauce

Slow cooking artichoke hearts gives them a velvety texture.

INGREDIENTS | SERVES 4

1 teaspoon olive oil

8 ounces frozen artichoke hearts, defrosted

3 cloves garlic, minced

1 medium onion, minced

2 tablespoons capote capers

1 (28-ounce) can crushed tomatoes

Cleaning Slow Cookers

Do not use very abrasive tools or cleansers on a slow cooker insert. They may scratch the surface, allowing bacteria and food to leach in. Use a soft sponge and baking soda for stubborn stains.

1. Heat the oil in a nonstick skillet over medium heat. Sauté the artichoke hearts, garlic, and onion for about 10–15 minutes, until the onion is translucent and most of the liquid has evaporated.

2. Put the mixture into a 4-quart slow cooker. Stir in the capers and crushed tomatoes.

3. Cook on high for 4 hours or on low for 8 hours.

PER SERVING: Calories: 24 | Fat: 1g | Protein: 0g | Sodium: 2mg | Fiber: 1g | Carbohydrates: 3g | Sugar: 1g

Pink Tomato Sauce

*Try this creamier version of classic spaghetti sauce over chicken and
a medley of oven-roasted vegetables.*

INGREDIENTS | SERVES 8

1 tablespoon olive oil

1 large onion, diced

2 cloves garlic, minced

1 tablespoon minced fresh basil

1 tablespoon minced fresh Italian parsley

⅔ cup coconut or almond milk

1 stalk celery, diced

16 ounces canned whole tomatoes in purée

28 ounces canned crushed tomatoes

1. Heat the olive oil in a medium-sized nonstick skillet over medium heat. Sauté the onion and garlic for 5–10 minutes, until the onion is soft.

2. Add the onion and garlic to a 6-quart slow cooker. Add the herbs, milk, celery, and tomatoes. Stir to distribute the spices. Cook on low for 10–12 hours.

PER SERVING: Calories: 62 | Fat: 6g | Protein: 1g | Sodium: 8mg | Fiber: 0g | Carbohydrates: 3g | Sugar: 1g

Celery, the Star

Celery is often overlooked as an ingredient. It is perfect for slow cooking because it has a high moisture content but still remains crisp through the cooking process. Celery is also very low in calories and high in fiber.

Tomato and Chicken Sausage Sauce

Sausage is a delicious alternative to meatballs in this rich tomato sauce.

INGREDIENTS | SERVES 6

4 Italian chicken sausages, sliced

2 tablespoons tomato paste

28 ounces canned crushed tomatoes

3 cloves garlic, minced

1 large onion, minced

3 tablespoons minced basil

1 tablespoon minced Italian parsley

¼ teaspoon crushed rosemary

¼ teaspoon freshly ground black pepper

1. Quickly brown the sausage slices on both sides in a nonstick skillet, about 1 minute on each side. Drain any grease.

2. Add the sausages to a 4-quart slow cooker, along with the remaining ingredients. Stir.

3. Cook on low for 8 hours.

PER SERVING: Calories: 82 | Fat: 2g | Protein: 13g | Sodium: 88mg | Fiber: 1g | Carbohydrates: 3g | Sugar: 1g

Chipotle Tomato Sauce

Try this southwestern take on the classic Italian tomato sauce for a Paleo "Pasta" (page 178),
or as salsa on a southwestern dish of choice.

INGREDIENTS | SERVES 6

3 cloves garlic, minced

1 large onion, minced

1 (28-ounce) can crushed tomatoes

1 (14-ounce) can diced tomatoes

3 chipotle peppers in adobo, minced

1 teaspoon dried oregano

1 tablespoon minced fresh cilantro

½ teaspoon freshly ground black pepper

Place all the ingredients into a 4-quart slow cooker. Cook on low for 8–10 hours. Stir before serving.

PER SERVING: Calories: 19 | Fat: 0g | Protein: 1g | Sodium: 3mg | Fiber: 1g | Carbohydrates: 4g | Sugar: 2g

Know Your Slow Cooker

When using a new or new-to-you slow cooker for the first time, pick a day when someone can be there to keep tabs on it. In general, older slow cookers cook at a higher temperature than new models, but even new slow cookers can have some differences. It is a good idea to know the quirks of a particular slow cooker so food is not overcooked or undercooked. Tweak cooking times accordingly.

Bolognese Sauce

Also called Bolognese or ragù alla Bolognese, this sauce combines vegetables and meat to create the perfect sauce for pouring over just about any beef and veggie dish, to give it a little touch of Italian.

INGREDIENTS | SERVES 6

2 teaspoons olive oil

½ pound 94% lean ground beef

½ pound ground pork

1 large onion, minced

1 large carrot, minced

1 stalk celery, minced

3 ounces tomato paste

28 ounces canned diced tomatoes

½ cup coconut or almond milk

¼ teaspoon freshly ground black pepper

⅛ teaspoon nutmeg

1. Heat the oil in a nonstick pan over medium heat. Brown the ground beef and pork, about 5–10 minutes. Drain off any excess fat.

2. Add the meats and the remaining ingredients to a 4-quart slow cooker. Cook on low for 8–10 hours. Stir before serving.

PER SERVING: Calories: 174 | Fat: 14g | Protein: 8g | Sodium: 148mg | Fiber: 1g | Carbohydrates: 6g | Sugar: 3g

Sun-Dried Tomato Sauce

Sun-dried tomatoes are an excellent source of lycopene, a micronutrient shown to be associated with cardiovascular health benefits and disease prevention.

INGREDIENTS | SERVES 4

1½ cups chopped sun-dried tomatoes

1 (28-ounce) can tomatoes, cut up

1 (14½-ounce) can tomatoes, cut up

1 medium onion, chopped

2 cloves garlic, minced

1 cup chopped celery

⅔ cup chablis or other dry white wine

1½ teaspoons basil

1 teaspoon dried fennel seed

½ teaspoon oregano

½ teaspoon freshly ground black pepper

8 ounces sliced mushrooms (optional)

Place all the ingredients in a 4- to 6-quart slow cooker, cover, and cook on low for 6–8 hours.

PER SERVING: Calories: 156 | Fat: 1g | Protein: 6g | Sodium: 877mg | Fiber: 7g | Carbohydrates: 29g | Sugar: 17g

Spinach Marinara Sauce

*Powerfully flavored and nutrient-rich. Goes well with chicken, beef, or turkey meatballs,
or as a sauce over a vegetable medley side dish or main course.*

INGREDIENTS | SERVES 8

1 (28-ounce) can peeled and crushed tomatoes, with liquid

1 (10-ounce) package frozen chopped spinach, thawed and drained

2⅔ (6-ounce) cans tomato paste

1 (4½-ounce) can sliced mushrooms, drained

1 medium onion, chopped

5 cloves garlic, minced

2 bay leaves

⅓ cup grated carrot

¼ cup olive oil

2½ tablespoons red pepper flakes

2 tablespoons lemon juice

2 tablespoons dried oregano

2 tablespoons dried basil

1. In a 4- to 6-quart slow cooker, combine all the ingredients, cover, and cook on high for 4 hours.

2. Stir, reduce heat to low, and cook for 1–2 more hours.

PER SERVING: Calories: 154 | Fat: 8g | Protein: 5g | Sodium: 482mg | Fiber: 6g | Carbohydrates: 21g | Sugar: 11g

Ground Turkey Tomato Sauce

Packed full of fresh, natural flavor—an excellent completion to just about any Italian dish.

INGREDIENTS | SERVES 6

2 tablespoons olive oil

1 pound ground turkey

1 (14½-ounce) can stewed tomatoes

1 (6-ounce) can tomato paste

½ teaspoon dried thyme

1 teaspoon dried basil

½ teaspoon oregano

½–1 teaspoon honey (optional)

1 yellow onion, chopped

1 bell pepper, chopped

2 cloves garlic, crushed

1 bay leaf

¼ cup water

4 ounces chopped or sliced mushrooms, fresh or canned, drained

1. Heat the olive oil in a skillet over medium heat. Add the ground turkey and cook for 5–7 minutes, until brown.

2. While browning turkey, place stewed tomatoes, tomato paste, thyme, basil, oregano, and honey in a 4- to 6-quart slow cooker. Stir well and turn on low heat.

3. Next, transfer browned turkey to slow cooker with slotted spoon. In pan with ground turkey drippings, sauté onion, pepper, garlic, and bay leaf for 3–5 minutes, until softened.

4. To slow cooker, add the sautéed vegetables, water, and the chopped mushrooms. Cover and cook on low for 4–6 hours. Thin with a little water if necessary.

PER SERVING: Calories: 211 | Fat: 13g | Protein: 15g | Sodium: 389mg | Fiber: 2g | Carbohydrates: 9g | Sugar: 5g

Cranberry Sauce

*Serve this sweet-tart cranberry sauce with a holiday meal;
use it as a spread, or pour it over your favorite slow-cooked dessert.*

INGREDIENTS | SERVES 10

12 ounces fresh cranberries

½ cup freshly squeezed orange juice

½ cup water

½ teaspoon orange zest

½ teaspoon agave nectar

Place all ingredients into a 1½- to 2-quart slow cooker. Cook on high for 2½ hours. Stir before serving.

PER SERVING: Calories: 16 | Fat: 0g | Protein: 0g | Sodium: 1mg | Fiber: 2g | Carbohydrates: 4g | Sugar: 1g

Cran-Apple Sauce

Simple. Sweet. Loaded with antioxidants like vitamin C.

INGREDIENTS | SERVES 6

1 cup fresh cranberries

8 apples, peeled, cored, and chopped

½ cup honey

1 cinnamon stick, halved

6 whole cloves

1. Combine cranberries, apples, and honey in a 4- to 6-quart slow cooker.

2. Place cinnamon and cloves in center of a 6" square of cheesecloth. Pull up around sides; tie to form pouch. Place in slow cooker.

3. Cover and cook on low for 4–5 hours or until cranberries and apples are very soft.

PER SERVING: (½ cup) | Calories: 197 | Fat: 0g | Protein: 1g | Sodium: 1mg | Fiber: 4g | Carbohydrates: 53g | Sugar: 46g

Mango Chutney

Chutney is a great complement to curry and meat dishes like pork, chicken, and fish.

INGREDIENTS | SERVES 4

4 cups peeled, finely chopped mangoes

3 cups peeled, finely chopped apples

1 cup golden raisins

1 cup honey

1 cup lemon juice

¼ teaspoon cinnamon

¼ teaspoon allspice

1. Combine all ingredients in a 4-quart slow cooker. Simmer on low for 4–5 hours. Stir often.

2. Serve warm as a spread on top of pork, chicken, or fish, or as a dip.

PER SERVING: (8 ounces) | Calories: 531 | Fat: 1g | Protein: 3g | Sodium: 40mg | Fiber: 6g | Carbohydrates: 139g | Sugar: 122g

Rosemary-Mushroom Sauce

Use as a marinade or sauce to enhance the flavor and texture of many slow-cooked beef and chicken dishes.

INGREDIENTS | SERVES 4

8 ounces fresh mushrooms, sliced

1 large onion, thinly sliced

1 teaspoon olive oil

1 tablespoon crushed rosemary

3 cups Chicken Stock (page 78)

1. In a sauté pan set over medium heat, sauté the mushrooms and onion in olive oil for about 5 minutes, until onion is soft.

2. Place onion and mushrooms into a 4-quart slow cooker; add the rosemary and stock, and stir.

3. Cook on low for 6–8 hours or on high for 3 hours.

PER SERVING: Calories: 133 | Fat: 4g | Protein: 8g | Sodium: 65mg | Fiber: 5g | Carbohydrates: 15g | Sugar: 6g

Awesome Applesauce

Serve warm or chilled, or as a complement to a main pork, chicken, or beef dish.
Or freeze for an icy, sweet summer treat!

INGREDIENTS | SERVES 6

3 pounds Jonathan apples, peeled and coarsely chopped

½ cup water

½ cup honey

Ground cinnamon, to taste

1. Combine all ingredients except cinnamon in a 6-quart slow cooker.

2. Cook on high, covered, until apples are very soft and form applesauce when stirred, about 2–2½ hours. Sprinkle with cinnamon just before serving.

PER SERVING: Calories: 86 | Fat: 0g | Protein: 0g | Sodium: 2mg | Fiber: 0g | Carbohydrates: 23g | Sugar: 23g

Slow-Cooked Spicy Salsa

Enjoy this salsa as a spicy, nutritious, low-calorie snack, or as a marinade
or complement to a slow-cooked southern dish.

INGREDIENTS | SERVES 16

10 fresh Roma or plum tomatoes, chopped

2 cloves garlic, minced

1 large onion, chopped

2 jalapeño peppers, chopped (remove seeds for milder salsa)

1 large green bell pepper, chopped

¼ cup fresh cilantro leaves

½ teaspoon lemon juice

1. Place chopped tomatoes, minced garlic, and chopped onion in a 3- to 4-quart slow cooker.

2. Stir jalapeño peppers and bell peppers into the slow cooker. Cover and cook on high for 2½–3 hours.

3. When cool, combine mixture with cilantro leaves and lemon juice and blend in a food processor to desired consistency.

PER SERVING: (½ cup) | Calories: 14 | Fat: 0g | Protein: 0g | Sodium: 3mg | Fiber: 1g | Carbohydrates: 3g | Sugar: 2g

Homemade Ketchup

Condiments such as ketchup are generally gluten-free, but you always have to read the label and check with the manufacturer to make sure. Instead of worrying, you can make your own and know exactly what ingredients are in your specially made ketchup!

INGREDIENTS | SERVES 5

1 (15-ounce) can no-salt-added tomato sauce

2 teaspoons water

½ teaspoon onion powder

¾ cup honey

⅓ cup lime juice

¼ teaspoon ground cinnamon

⅛ teaspoon ground cloves

Pinch ground allspice

Pinch nutmeg

Pinch freshly ground black pepper

⅔ teaspoon sweet paprika

Ketchup with a Kick

If you like zesty ketchup, you can add crushed red peppers or salt-free chili powder along with, or instead of, the cinnamon and other seasonings. Another alternative is to use hot paprika rather than sweet paprika.

1. Add all the ingredients to a 2½-quart slow cooker. Cover and, stirring occasionally, cook on low for 2–4 hours or until ketchup reaches desired consistency.

2. Turn off the slow cooker or remove the insert from the slow cooker. Allow mixture to cool, then put in a covered container (such as a recycled ketchup bottle). Store in the refrigerator for up to a month.

PER SERVING: (½ cup) | Calories: 156 | Fat: 0g | Protein: 0g | Sodium: 2mg | Fiber: 0g | Carbohydrates: 42g | Sugar: 42g

Plum Sauce

Plum sauce is usually served with egg rolls, which are generally not Paleo-approved. But this delicious sauce is also wonderful brushed on chicken or pork ribs; doing so near the end of the grilling time will add a succulent glaze to the grilled meat.

INGREDIENTS | SERVES 16

8 cups (about 3 pounds) plums, pitted and cut in half

1 small sweet onion, finely diced

1 cup water

1 teaspoon fresh ginger, peeled and minced

1 clove garlic, peeled and minced

¾ cup honey

½ cup lemon juice

1 teaspoon ground coriander

½ teaspoon cinnamon

¼ teaspoon cayenne pepper

¼ teaspoon ground cloves

1. Add the plums, onion, water, ginger, and garlic to a 4-quart slow cooker. Cover and, stirring occasionally, cook on low for 4 hours or until plums and onions are tender.

2. Use an immersion blender to pulverize the contents of the slow cooker before straining it or press the cooked plum mixture through a sieve.

3. Return the liquefied and strained plum mixture to the slow cooker and stir in honey, lemon juice, coriander, cinnamon, cayenne pepper, and cloves. Cover and, stirring occasionally, cook on low for 2 hours or until the sauce reaches the consistency of applesauce.

PER SERVING: Calories: 91 | Fat: 0g | Protein: 1g | Sodium: 3mg | Fiber: 1g | Carbohydrates: 24g | Sugar: 22g

Red Pepper Relish

This sauce adds a little kick, spicing up the flavor in just about any slow-cooked entrée or side.

INGREDIENTS | SERVES 8

4 large red bell peppers, cut into thin strips

2 small Vidalia onions, thinly sliced

6 tablespoons lemon juice

¼ cup honey

½ teaspoon dried thyme

½ teaspoon red pepper flakes

½ teaspoon freshly ground black pepper

1. Combine all the ingredients in a 1½-quart slow cooker and mix well.

2. Cover and cook on low for 4 hours.

PER SERVING: Calories: 61 | Fat: 0g | Protein: 1g | Sodium: 6mg | Fiber: 2g | Carbohydrates: 15g | Sugar: 12g

Paleo "Butterscotch-Caramel" Sauce

Here is a sweet and delicious way to enhance the flavor of just about any Paleo dessert.

INGREDIENTS | SERVES 24

½ cup coconut butter

2 cups (full-fat) coconut milk

3 cups honey

2 tablespoons fresh lemon juice

1 tablespoon vanilla extract

1. Add the coconut butter, coconut milk, honey, and lemon juice to a 2-quart or smaller slow cooker. Cover and cook on high for 1 hour or until the coconut butter is melted and the milk begins to bubble around the edges of the cooker. Uncover and stir.

2. Cover and cook on low for 2 hours, stirring occasionally.

3. Uncover and cook on low for 1 more hour or until the mixture coats the back of the spoon or the sauce reaches the desired thickness. Stir in the vanilla.

PER SERVING: Calories: 168 | Fat: 4g | Protein: 1g | Sodium: 5mg | Fiber: 0g | Carbohydrates: 36g | Sugar: 35g

Chapter 5

Stocks, Soups, and Stews

Chicken Stock

Homemade chicken stock is much cheaper and tastier than store-bought.

INGREDIENTS | YIELDS 3 QUARTS

1 (5–7 pound) chicken carcass

2 large carrots, peeled and cut into chunks

2 stalks celery, cut into chunks

2 medium onions, cut into chunks

2 parsnips, cut into chunks

1 head garlic

2 chicken wings

Water, as needed

Stock Options

Any leftover vegetables can be added to stock for extra flavor; fennel fronds, green onions, turnips, and red onion are all good choices. Depending on the recipe that the stock will be used in, adding items like dried chilies, ginger, or galangal root will customize the stock, making it an even better fit for the final product.

1. Place the carcass, carrots, celery, onions, parsnips, garlic, and wings into a 6-quart slow cooker.

2. Fill the slow cooker with water until it is 2 inches below the top. Cover and cook on low for 10 hours.

3. Strain into a large container. Discard the solids. Refrigerate the stock overnight.

4. The next day, scoop off any fat that has floated to the top. Discard the fat.

5. Freeze or refrigerate the stock and use within 1 week.

PER SERVING: (1 cup) | Calories: 31 | Fat: 1g | Protein: 2g | Sodium: 20mg | Fiber: 1g | Carbohydrates: 3g | Sugar: 1g

Beef Stock

A flavorful, easy-to-prepare stock, suitable for a variety of recipes.

INGREDIENTS | YIELDS 2 QUARTS

8 black peppercorns

5 sage leaves

4 large onions, thickly sliced

4 medium carrots, thickly sliced

4 small stalks celery, thickly sliced

2½ quarts water

2 ribs from cooked beef rib roast, fat trimmed

2 bay leaves

1 parsnip, peeled and sliced

1. Combine all the ingredients in a 6-quart slow cooker. Cover and cook on low for 6–8 hours.

2. Strain the stock through a double layer of cheesecloth, discarding the solids.

3. Refrigerate 2–3 hours, until chilled. Remove fat from surface of stock.

4. Freeze or refrigerate the stock and use within 1 week.

PER SERVING: (1 cup) | Calories: 46 | Fat: 0g | Protein: 1g | Sodium: 49mg | Fiber: 2g | Carbohydrates: 11g | Sugar: 5g

Roasted Vegetable Stock

Use this stock in vegetarian recipes as a substitute for chicken stock,
or in other recipes as a flavorful alternative to water.

INGREDIENTS | YIELDS 5 QUARTS

3 medium carrots, peeled and coarsely chopped

3 parsnips, peeled and coarsely chopped

3 large onions, quartered

3 whole turnips

3 rutabagas, quartered

3 bell peppers, halved

2 shallots

1 whole head garlic

1 bunch fresh thyme

1 bunch parsley

5 quarts water

1. Preheat the oven to 425°F. Arrange the vegetables and herbs in a 9" × 13" baking pan lined with parchment paper. Roast for 30 minutes or until browned.

2. Add the vegetables to a 6-quart slow cooker. Add 5 quarts water and cover. Cook on low for 8–10 hours. Strain the stock, discarding the solids. Freeze or refrigerate the stock and use within 1–2 weeks.

PER SERVING: (1 cup) | Calories: 46 | Fat: 0g | Protein: 1g | Sodium: 49mg | Fiber: 2g | Carbohydrates: 11g | Sugar: 5g

Turkey Stock

Popular during the holidays, this is the perfect way to put your leftover turkey to good use.
This can also be used as a substitute in recipes calling for chicken stock.

INGREDIENTS | YIELDS 16 CUPS

10 black peppercorns

6 sprigs parsley

4 medium carrots, thickly sliced

4 stalks celery, thickly sliced

4 quarts water

2 medium onions, thickly sliced

2 leeks, white parts only

1 turkey carcass, cut up

1 cup dry white wine or water

1½ teaspoons dried thyme

Freshly ground black pepper, to taste

1. Combine all the ingredients except pepper in a 6-quart slow cooker. Cover and cook on low for 6–8 hours.

2. Strain the stock through a double layer of cheesecloth, discarding the solids. Season with pepper to taste.

3. Refrigerate 3–5 hours, until chilled. Remove fat from surface of stock.

4. Freeze or refrigerate the stock and use within 1 week.

PER SERVING: (1 cup) | Calories: 33 | Fat: 0g | Protein: 1g | Sodium: 29mg | Fiber: 1g | Carbohydrates: 5g | Sugar: 2g

Fish Stock

Use this fish stock in any fish or seafood dish instead of water or chicken stock.

INGREDIENTS | YIELDS 3 QUARTS

3 quarts water

2 large onions, quartered

Head and bones from 3 fish, any type

2 stalks celery, chopped

2 tablespoons peppercorns

1 bunch parsley

1. Place all the ingredients into a 4-quart slow cooker. Cook for 8–10 hours.

2. Remove all the solids. Refrigerate overnight.

3. The next day, skim off any foam that has floated to the top. Refrigerate and use within 1 week, or freeze.

PER SERVING: (1 cup) | Calories: 33 | Fat: 0g | Protein: 1g | Sodium: 29mg | Fiber: 1g | Carbohydrates: 5g | Sugar: 2g

Mushroom Stock

Shiitake mushrooms add a rich, bold flavor and also provide a variety of beneficial phytonutrients. Be careful to not overcook this stock.

INGREDIENTS | YIELDS 2 QUARTS

1 quart water

12 ounces white mushrooms

6 sprigs parsley

1 large onion, sliced

1 leek, white part only

1 stalk celery, sliced

2 ounces dried shiitake mushrooms

1 tablespoon minced garlic

1½ teaspoons black peppercorns

¾ teaspoon dried sage

¾ teaspoon dried thyme

Freshly ground black pepper, to taste

1. Combine all the ingredients except pepper in a 6-quart slow cooker; cover and cook on low for 6–8 hours.

2. Strain, discarding solids; season to taste with pepper. Serve immediately, refrigerate and use within 1–2 weeks, or freeze.

PER SERVING: (1 cup) | Calories: 18 | Fat: 0g | Protein: 1g | Sodium: 11mg | Fiber: 1g | Carbohydrates: 4g | Sugar: 1g

Beef and Vegetable Stew

Fresh herbs brighten this traditional hearty stew. This recipe could be prepared with a variety of seasonal herbs—experiment for yourself!

INGREDIENTS | SERVES 4

2 teaspoons canola oil

1 large onion, diced

2 parsnips, diced

2 large carrots, peeled and diced

2 stalks celery, diced

3 cloves garlic, minced

1 tablespoon minced fresh tarragon

2 tablespoons minced fresh rosemary

1 pound lean beef top round roast, cut into 1-inch cubes

1½ cups water

1 bulb fennel, diced

1 tablespoon minced parsley

1. Heat the oil in a large skillet. Sauté the onion, parsnips, carrots, celery, garlic, tarragon, rosemary, and beef for 5–10 minutes, until the ingredients begin to soften and brown. Drain off any excess fat.

2. Place the mixture into a 4-quart slow cooker. Pour in the water. Stir. Cook on low for 8–9 hours.

3. Add the fennel. Cover and cook on high for an additional ½ hour. Stir in the parsley before serving.

PER SERVING: Calories: 227 | Fat: 7g | Protein: 27g | Sodium: 145mg | Fiber: 4g | Carbohydrates: 13g | Sugar: 4g

Bouillabaisse

*With one bite, this slightly simplified version of the Provençal fish stew will convert anyone
who is skeptical about cooking seafood in the slow cooker into a believer.*

INGREDIENTS | SERVES 8

1 bulb fennel, sliced

2 leeks, sliced

2 large carrots, peeled and cut into coins

2 shallots, minced

5 cloves garlic, minced

2 tablespoons minced basil

1 tablespoon orange zest

1 tablespoon lemon zest

1 bay leaf

1 (14½-ounce) can diced tomatoes

2 quarts water or Fish Stock (page 80)

1 pound cubed hake or catfish

8 ounces medium peeled shrimp

1 pound mussels

1. Place the vegetables, garlic, basil, zests, bay leaf, tomatoes, and water or stock into a 6-quart slow cooker. Stir. Cook on low for 8 hours.

2. Add the seafood. Cook on high for 20 minutes. Stir prior to serving. Discard any mussels that do not open.

PER SERVING: Calories: 251 | Fat: 3.5g | Protein: 27g | Sodium: 384mg | Fiber: 8g | Carbohydrates: 31g | Sugar: 9g

Curried Cauliflower Soup

Orange cauliflower is an excellent variety to use in this recipe. It has 25 percent more vitamin A than white cauliflower and lends an attractive color to the soup.

INGREDIENTS | SERVES 4

1 pound cauliflower florets

2½ cups water

1 medium onion, minced

2 cloves garlic, minced

3 teaspoons curry powder

¼ teaspoon cumin

Curry Powder Power

Curry powder is a mixture of spices commonly used in South Asian cooking. While it does not correlate directly to any particular kind of curry, it is popular in Europe and North America to add an Indian flare to dishes. It can contain any number of spices, but nearly always includes turmeric, which gives it its distinctive yellow color.

1. Place all the ingredients into a 4-quart slow cooker. Stir. Cook on low for 8 hours.

2. Use an immersion blender to blend until smooth, or blend the soup in batches in a standard blender.

PER SERVING: Calories: 46 | Fat: 1g | Protein: 3g | Sodium: 40mg | Fiber: 3g | Carbohydrates: 10g | Sugar: 3g

No Bean Chili

For a variation, try this with lean beef sirloin instead of pork.

INGREDIENTS | SERVES 6

1 tablespoon canola oil

1 pound boneless pork tenderloin, cubed

1 large onion, diced

3 poblano chilies, diced

2 cloves garlic, minced

1 teaspoon cumin

1 teaspoon dried oregano

1 cup Chicken Stock (page 78)

15 ounces canned crushed tomatoes

2 teaspoons cayenne pepper

Using Herbs

As a general rule, 1 tablespoon minced fresh herbs equals 1 teaspoon dried herbs. Fresh herbs can be frozen for future use. Discard dried herbs after one year.

1. In a large nonstick skillet, heat the oil over medium heat. Add the pork, onion, chilies, and garlic. Sauté for 7–10 minutes, until the pork is no longer visibly pink on any side. Drain off any fats or oils and discard them.

2. Place the pork mixture into a 4-quart slow cooker. Add the remaining ingredients. Stir.

3. Cook on low for 8–9 hours.

PER SERVING: Calories: 157 | Fat: 5g | Protein: 19g | Sodium: 64mg | Fiber: 2g | Carbohydrates: 5g | Sugar: 2g

Mushroom and Onion Soup

This soup serves as an excellent opening course for a rich beef or pork dish.

INGREDIENTS | SERVES 6

6½ cups Chicken Stock (page 78)

3 cups thinly sliced onions

2 cups fresh mushrooms, sliced

1½ cups thinly sliced leeks

½ cup chopped shallots or green onions

1 teaspoon honey (optional)

Freshly ground black pepper, to taste

1. Combine all the ingredients except the pepper in a 6-quart slow cooker. Cover and cook on low 6–8 hours.

2. Season with pepper to taste.

PER SERVING: Calories: 191 | Fat: 4g | Protein: 11g | Sodium: 404mg | Fiber: 3g | Carbohydrates: 27g | Sugar: 12g

Acorn Squash Autumn Bisque

A seasonally delicious taste of fall. The yellow-orange color of squash is derived from its rich content of vitamin A. One cup of acorn squash provides more than 100 percent of the daily recommended amount of vitamin A.

INGREDIENTS | SERVES 6

2 cups Chicken Stock (page 78)

2 medium acorn squash, peeled and cut into cubes

½ cup chopped onion

½ teaspoon ground cinnamon

¼ teaspoon ground coriander

¼ teaspoon ground cumin

½ cup unsweetened coconut milk

1 tablespoon lemon juice

Freshly ground black pepper, to taste

1. Combine the stock, squash, onion, cinnamon, coriander, and cumin in a 4-quart slow cooker. Cover and cook on high for 3–4 hours.

2. Blend the soup, coconut milk, and lemon juice in food processor until smooth.

3. Season with pepper to taste.

PER SERVING: Calories: 54 | Fat: 4g | Protein: 2g | Sodium: 11mg | Fiber: 1g | Carbohydrates: 3g | Sugar: 1g

Pumpkin Turkey Chili

Pumpkin keeps for 6 months whole, or for years canned; pumpkin is most often enjoyed in the fall, but can actually be enjoyed all year round.

INGREDIENTS | SERVES 6

2 red bell peppers, chopped

1 medium onion, chopped

3–4 cloves garlic, chopped

1 pound ground turkey, browned

1 (14½-ounce) can pure pumpkin purée

1 (14½-ounce) can diced tomatoes

½ cup water

1½ tablespoons chili powder

½ teaspoon freshly ground black pepper

¼ teaspoon cumin

1. In a skillet over medium heat, sauté the peppers, onion, and garlic with the browned turkey for 5–7 minutes.

2. Transfer the turkey and veggies into a 4-quart slow cooker. Add the remaining ingredients.

3. Cover and cook on low for 5–6 hours.

PER SERVING: Calories: 140 | Fat: 7g | Protein: 14g | Sodium: 188mg | Fiber: 2g | Carbohydrates: 6g | Sugar: 2g

Chicken and Mushroom Stew

A fragrant blend of sautéed chicken, vegetables, and herbs, best enjoyed on a late autumn night alongside a rich poultry dish.

INGREDIENTS | SERVES 6

16–24 ounces boneless chicken, cut into 1-inch cubes and browned in olive oil

8 ounces fresh mushrooms, sliced

1 medium onion, diced

3 cups diced zucchini

1 cup diced green pepper

4 cloves garlic, minced

1 tablespoon olive oil

3 medium tomatoes, diced

1 (6-ounce) can tomato paste

¾ cup water

1 teaspoon each: dried thyme, oregano, marjoram, and basil

1. Add browned chicken to a 4- to 6-quart slow cooker.

2. In a sauté pan over medium heat, sauté the mushrooms, onion, zucchini, green pepper, and garlic in olive oil for 5–10 minutes, until crisp-tender. Add to slow cooker.

3. Add the tomatoes, tomato paste, water, and seasonings.

4. Cover and cook on low for 4 hours or until the vegetables are tender. Serve hot.

PER SERVING: Calories: 222 | Fat: 6g | Protein: 28g | Sodium: 320mg | Fiber: 4g | Carbohydrates: 15g | Sugar: 9g

Southwestern Soup

A zesty and hearty creation with the perfect balance of herbs and seasonings.

INGREDIENTS | SERVES 4

1 pound pork tenderloin, cut into 1-inch pieces

1 cup chopped onion

1 green bell pepper, seeded and chopped

1 jalapeño pepper, seeded and minced

2 cloves garlic, minced

1 teaspoon chili powder

1 teaspoon ground cumin

¼ teaspoon freshly ground black pepper

5 cups Chicken Stock (page 78)

1 (14½-ounce) can diced tomatoes

1 cup diced fresh avocado, for garnish

2 tablespoons chopped fresh cilantro, for garnish

Lime wedges, for garnish

1. In the bottom of a 6-quart slow cooker, combine the pork, onion, bell pepper, jalapeño pepper, garlic, chili powder, cumin, and black pepper. Stir to combine.

2. Add stock and tomatoes. Cover and cook on low for 6–8 hours or on high for 3–4 hours.

3. When ready to serve, ladle soup into bowls and top with avocado and cilantro. Garnish soup with lime wedges.

PER SERVING: Calories: 266 | Fat: 9g | Protein: 29g | Sodium: 237mg | Fiber: 6g | Carbohydrates: 18g | Sugar: 6g

Tomato Vegetable Soup

The array of garden vegetables in this soup produces a light and fresh flavor with a "fall-ish" feel.

INGREDIENTS | SERVES 6

1 (28-ounce) can Italian plum tomatoes, undrained

2¼ cups beef broth

1 medium onion, chopped

1 large stalk celery, sliced

1 medium carrot, sliced

1 red bell pepper, chopped

1 teaspoon lemon juice

¾ teaspoon garlic powder

Pinch of red pepper flakes

Freshly ground black pepper, to taste

1. Combine all the ingredients except pepper in a 4- to 6-quart slow cooker. Cover and cook on high for 4–5 hours.

2. Process the soup in blender until smooth; season to taste with pepper. Serve warm.

PER SERVING: Calories: 50 | Fat: 1g | Protein: 3g | Sodium: 314mg | Fiber: 3g | Carbohydrates: 10g | Sugar: 6g

Zucchini Soup

This smooth and soothing blend of fresh herbs and spices is perfect for a cold, late-autumn day.

INGREDIENTS | SERVES 8

4 cups sliced zucchini

4 cups chicken broth

4 cloves garlic, minced

2 tablespoons lime juice

2 teaspoons curry powder

1 teaspoon dried marjoram

¼ teaspoon celery seeds

½ cup coconut milk

Cayenne pepper, to taste

Pinch of paprika

1. Combine all the ingredients except the coconut milk, cayenne pepper, and paprika in a 4- to 6-quart slow cooker. Cook on high for 3–4 hours.

2. Process the soup and coconut milk in a blender until combined.

3. Season to taste with cayenne pepper. Serve warm, and sprinkle with paprika.

PER SERVING: Calories: 92 | Fat: 5g | Protein: 4g | Sodium: 531mg | Fiber: 1g | Carbohydrates: 9g | Sugar: 2g

Pumpkin and Ginger Soup

Relieve some stress with a hot cup of this comforting, seasonal favorite.

INGREDIENTS | SERVES 6

2 pounds pumpkin, peeled, seeded, and cut into cubes

3 cups chicken stock

1 cup chopped onion

½ cup dry white wine

1 tablespoon chopped ginger root

1 teaspoon minced garlic

½ teaspoon ground cloves

Freshly ground black pepper, to taste

1. In a 4-quart slow cooker, combine all ingredients except the pepper. Cover and cook on high for 4–5 hours.

2. Place the soup in a food processor and blend until smooth.

3. Season to taste with pepper.

PER SERVING: Calories: 84 | Fat: 1g | Protein: 3g | Sodium: 14mg | Fiber: 2g | Carbohydrates: 15g | Sugar: 4g

Rosemary-Thyme Stew

Lots of rosemary and thyme give this surprisingly light stew a distinctive flavor.

INGREDIENTS | SERVES 4

1 teaspoon canola oil

1 large onion, diced

1 large carrot, peeled and diced

2 stalks celery, diced

2 cloves garlic, minced

3½ tablespoons minced fresh thyme

3 tablespoons minced fresh rosemary

1 pound boneless, skinless chicken breasts, cut into 1-inch cubes

½ teaspoon freshly ground black pepper

1½ cups water or Chicken Stock (page 78)

1 cup diced green, red, and yellow bell peppers

1. Heat the oil in a large skillet. Sauté the onion, carrot, celery, garlic, thyme, rosemary, and chicken for 5–7 minutes, until the chicken is white on all sides. Drain off any excess fat.

2. Put sautéed ingredients into a 4-quart slow cooker. Sprinkle with black pepper. Pour in the water or stock. Stir. Cook on low for 8–9 hours.

3. Add the diced peppers. Cover and cook on high for an additional ½ hour. Stir before serving.

PER SERVING: Calories: 187 | Fat: 4g | Protein: 26g | Sodium: 173mg | Fiber: 3g | Carbohydrates: 10g | Sugar: 3g

Chicken Stew with Meat Sauce

This easy-to-make chicken stew is sure to please the entire family. Both kids and adults love this delicious recipe. Serve alone or pour over spaghetti squash as a Bolognese-type sauce.

INGREDIENTS | SERVES 4

1 pound 90% lean grass-fed ground beef

4 boneless, skinless chicken breasts

1 (6-ounce) can organic tomato paste

1 (28-ounce) can diced organic tomatoes, no salt added

4 cloves garlic, chopped

4 large carrots, sliced

2 red bell peppers, diced

2 green bell peppers, diced

1 tablespoon dried thyme

2 tablespoons olive oil

1 tablespoon chili powder

Slow Cookers Are Lifesavers

Slow cookers are the greatest appliance for the Paleo enthusiast. These little counter-top cookers allow you to cook easily and in bulk, which is important for a successful Paleolithic dieter.

1. In a medium sauté pan, cook ground beef until browned, about 5 minutes. Drain and place in a 4- to 6-quart slow cooker.

2. Wipe out the sauté pan and place it over medium-high heat. Brown the chicken breasts, about 5 minutes per side. Add to slow cooker.

3. Combine all the remaining ingredients in the slow cooker. Cook on high for 5 hours.

4. Serve over your favorite steamed vegetable.

PER SERVING: Calories: 469 | Fat: 14g | Protein: 56g | Sodium: 960mg | Fiber: 9g | Carbohydrates: 32g | Sugar: 17g

Simple Ground Turkey and Vegetable Soup

This soup is easy to throw together with pantry ingredients.

INGREDIENTS | SERVES 6

1 tablespoon olive oil

1 pound ground turkey

1 medium onion, diced

2 cloves garlic, minced

1 (16-ounce) package frozen mixed vegetables

4 cups chicken broth

½ teaspoon freshly ground black pepper

1. In a large skillet over medium heat, add olive oil and heat until sizzling. Cook ground turkey until browned, about 5–6 minutes, stirring to break up the meat. Add meat to a greased 4-quart slow cooker.

2. In the same skillet, sauté onion and garlic until softened, about 3–5 minutes. Add to the slow cooker.

3. Add remaining ingredients. Cover and cook on high for 4 hours or on low for 8 hours.

PER SERVING: Calories: 254 | Fat: 11g | Protein: 19g | Sodium: 804mg | Fiber: 3g | Carbohydrates: 20g | Sugar: 1g

Stuffed Pepper Soup

All the flavor of stuffed peppers turned into a warm and satisfying soup.

INGREDIENTS | SERVES 6

1½ pounds ground beef, browned and drained

3 cups diced green bell peppers

2 cups diced butternut squash

1 (28-ounce) can diced peeled tomatoes

1 (28-ounce) can tomato sauce

¾ cup honey

Seasonings of choice, to taste: e.g. basil, thyme, oregano, onion flakes, etc.

1. Mix all the ingredients in a 4-quart slow cooker. Cover and cook on low for 3–4 hours or until the green peppers are cooked.

2. Turn heat to high and cook for 20–30 more minutes.

PER SERVING: Calories: 415 | Fat: 12g | Protein: 26g | Sodium: 951mg | Fiber: 6g | Carbohydrates: 56g | Sugar: 46g

Cincinnati Chili

This unusual regional favorite has a spicy-sweet flavor that is wonderfully addictive! Serve over cooked Paleo "Pasta" (page 178) with any combination of the following toppings: diced raw onion, chopped green, red, yellow, or orange pepper, and shredded carrots.

INGREDIENTS | SERVES 8

1 pound ground beef

15 ounces crushed tomatoes in juice

2 cloves garlic, minced

1 large onion, diced

1 teaspoon cumin

1 teaspoon cacao powder

2 teaspoons chili powder

½ teaspoon ground cloves

1 tablespoon lemon juice

1 teaspoon allspice

½ teaspoon cayenne pepper

½ teaspoon cinnamon

Sauté the Meat When Making Chili

Even though it is not aesthetically necessary to brown the meat when making chili, sautéing meat before adding it to the slow cooker allows you to drain off any extra fat. Not only is it healthier to cook with less fat, your chili will be unappetizingly greasy if there is too much fat present in the meat during cooking.

1. In a nonstick skillet, quickly sauté the beef until it is no longer pink, about 5–6 minutes. Drain and discard all fat.

2. Place beef and all the other ingredients in a 4-quart slow cooker. Stir. Cook on low for 8–10 hours.

PER SERVING: Calories: 110 | Fat: 6g | Protein: 12g | Sodium: 45mg | Fiber: 1g | Carbohydrates: 3g | Sugar: 1g

Lone Star State Chili

Texans prefer their chili without beans, so this recipe is perfect for the Paleo diet. Serve this dish with a tossed salad.

INGREDIENTS | SERVES 8

1 stalk celery, finely chopped

1 large carrot, peeled and finely chopped

1 (3-pound) chuck roast, cut into small cubes

2 large yellow onions, peeled and diced

6 cloves garlic, peeled and minced

6 jalapeño peppers, seeded and diced

½ teaspoon freshly ground black pepper

4 tablespoons chili powder

1 teaspoon Mexican oregano

1 teaspoon ground cumin

1 teaspoon honey

1 (28-ounce) can diced tomatoes

1 cup beef broth

1. Add all of the ingredients to a 4- to 6-quart slow cooker, in the order given, and stir to combine. The liquid in your slow cooker should completely cover the meat and vegetables. If additional liquid is needed, add more crushed tomatoes, broth, or some water.

2. Cover and cook on low for 8 hours. Taste for seasoning, and add more chili powder if desired.

PER SERVING: Calories: 60 | Fat: 1g | Protein: 2g | Sodium: 289mg | Fiber: 4g | Carbohydrates: 13g | Sugar: 6g

Hot Pepper Precautions

Wear gloves or sandwich bags over your hands when you clean and dice hot peppers. It's important to avoid having the peppers come into contact with any of your skin, and especially your eyes. As an added precaution, wash your hands (and under your fingernails) thoroughly with hot soapy water after you remove the gloves or sandwich bags.

Chicken Chili Verde

*Enjoy this spicy chili over a southwestern-themed vegetable medley.
Avocado slices serve well as a festive garnish.*

INGREDIENTS | SERVES 8

½ tablespoon olive oil

2 pounds skinless, boneless chicken breasts, cubed

2 (28-ounce) cans whole peeled tomatoes, undrained

1 (4-ounce) can diced green chili peppers, undrained

1 teaspoon thyme

1 teaspoon oregano

1 teaspoon basil

1 tablespoon chili powder

2 teaspoons cumin

1 tablespoon honey

1 large onion, minced

3 cloves garlic, minced

½ cup water

1. Heat oil in a skillet over medium heat. Add the chicken. Cook, stirring frequently, until chicken is browned on all sides, about 1–2 minutes per side. Place browned chicken in a greased 4- to 6-quart slow cooker.

2. Add the remaining ingredients over the chicken in the slow cooker.

3. Cover and cook on high for 3 hours or on low for 6 hours.

PER SERVING: Calories: 195 | Fat: 4g | Protein: 26g | Sodium: 423mg | Fiber: 3g | Carbohydrates: 14g | Sugar: 8g

Paleo "Cream" of Mushroom Soup

This Paleo-approved "cream" of mushroom soup is a simple and light main dish. It's also a perfect Paleo-friendly base to use when a recipe calls for canned cream soup.

INGREDIENTS | SERVES 4

2 tablespoons canola oil

2 tablespoons coconut butter

1 cup finely diced fresh mushrooms

4 tablespoons arrowroot powder

2 cups (full-fat) coconut milk

½ teaspoon freshly ground black pepper

Cream Soup Variations

You can make any number of homemade cream soups with this recipe. If you would rather have cream of celery soup, use 1 cup finely diced celery instead of the mushrooms. For a cream of chicken soup, use 1 cup finely diced chicken and 2 teaspoons poultry seasoning.

1. Heat the oil and coconut butter in a deep saucepan until sizzling. Add the diced mushrooms and cook until soft, approximately 4–5 minutes.

2. In a medium bowl, whisk the arrowroot powder into the coconut milk. Slowly add to the mushrooms. Cook on medium heat for 5–10 minutes, whisking consistently, until slightly thickened.

3. Carefully pour cream soup into a greased 2½-quart slow cooker. Add pepper and any additional seasonings you would like. Cook on high for 2 hours or on low for 4 hours.

PER SERVING: Calories: 312 | Fat: 31g | Protein: 2g | Sodium: 15mg | Fiber: 0g | Carbohydrates: 10g | Sugar: 0g

Brown Stock

When you add ¼ cup of this concentrated broth to a slow-cooked beef dish, you'll get the same succulent flavor as if you had first seared the meat in a hot skillet before adding it to the slow cooker. The broth also gives a delicious flavor boost to slow-cooked tomato sauce or tomato gravy.

INGREDIENTS | YIELDS ABOUT 4 CUPS

2 large carrots, scrubbed

2 stalks celery

1½ pounds bone-in chuck roast

1½ pounds cracked beef bones

1 large onion, peeled and quartered

Freshly ground black pepper, to taste

4½ cups water

1. Preheat the oven to 450°F. Cut the carrots and celery into large pieces. Put them, along with the meat, bones, and onion, into a roasting pan. Season with pepper. Put the pan in the middle part of the oven and, turning the meat and vegetables occasionally, roast for 45 minutes or until evenly browned.

2. Transfer the roasted meat, bones, and vegetables to a 4- or 6-quart slow cooker. Add the water to the roasting pan; scrape any browned bits clinging to the pan and then pour the water into the slow cooker. Cover and cook on low for 8 hours. (It may be necessary to skim accumulated fat and scum from the top of the pan juices; check the broth after 4 hours and again after 6 hours to see if that's needed.)

3. Use a slotted spoon to remove the roast and beef bones. Reserve the roast and the meat removed from the bones for another use; discard the bones.

4. Once the broth has cooled enough to handle, strain it; discard the cooked vegetables. Refrigerate the (cooled) broth overnight. Remove and discard the hardened fat. The resulting concentrated broth can be kept for 1 or 2 days in the refrigerator, or frozen for up to 3 months.

PER SERVING: (1 cup) | Calories: 33 | Fat: 0g | Protein: 1g | Sodium: 50mg | Fiber: 2g | Carbohydrates: 8g | Sugar: 4g

Pork Broth

Pork broth is seldom called for in recipes, but it can add layers of flavor when mixed with chicken broth in vegetable soups.

INGREDIENTS | YIELDS ABOUT 4 CUPS

1 (3-pound) bone-in pork butt roast
1 large onion, peeled and quartered
12 baby carrots
2 stalks celery, cut in half
4½ cups water

Pork Roast Dinner

To make concentrated broth and a pork roast dinner at the same time, increase the amount of carrots, decrease the water to 2½ cups, and add 4 peeled, medium sweet potatoes (cut in half) on top. Cook on low for 6 hours.

1. Add all the ingredients to a 4-quart slow cooker. Cover and cook on low for 6 hours or until the pork is tender and pulls away from the bone.

2. Strain; discard the celery and onion. Reserve the pork roast and carrots for another use. Once cooled, cover and refrigerate the broth overnight. Remove and discard the hardened fat. The broth can be kept for 1 or 2 days in the refrigerator, or frozen for up to 3 months.

PER SERVING: (1 cup) | Calories: 29 | Fat: 0g | Protein: 1g | Sodium: 49mg | Fiber: 2g | Carbohydrates: 7g | Sugar: 3g

Seafood Stock

This recipe calls for using the shells only because the amount of time it takes to slow cook the stock would result in seafood that would be too tough to eat.

INGREDIENTS | YIELDS ABOUT 4 CUPS

2 pounds large or jumbo shrimp, crab, or lobster shells
1 large onion, peeled and thinly sliced
1 tablespoon fresh lemon juice
4 cups water

Fish or Seafood Stock in a Hurry

For each cup of seafood or fish stock called for in a recipe, you can substitute ¼ cup of bottled clam juice and ¾ cup of water. Just keep in mind that the clam juice is very salty, so adjust any recipe in which you use it accordingly.

1. Add the seafood shells, onion, lemon juice, and water, to a 4-quart slow cooker. Cover and cook on low for 4–8 hours.

2. Strain through a fine sieve or fine wire-mesh strainer. Discard the shells and onions. Refrigerate in a covered container and use within 2 days or freeze for up to 3 months.

PER SERVING: (1 cup) | Calories: 253 | Fat: 4g | Protein: 46g | Sodium: 341mg | Fiber: 1g | Carbohydrates: 6g | Sugar: 2g

Paleo "Cream" of Broccoli Soup

This Paleo-approved "cream" soup serves as a light meal on its own, or can be poured over a chicken or vegetable dish to enhance flavor and richness.

INGREDIENTS | SERVES 4

1 (12-ounce) package frozen broccoli florets, thawed
1 small onion, peeled and diced
4 cups chicken broth
Freshly ground black pepper, to taste
1 cup (full-fat) coconut milk

1. Add the broccoli, onion, broth, and pepper to a 2- or 4-quart slow cooker; cover and cook on low for 4 hours.

2. Use an immersion blender to purée the soup. Stir in the coconut milk. Cover and cook on low for 30 minutes, stirring occasionally, until the soup is heated through.

PER SERVING: Calories: 241 | Fat: 16g | Protein: 8g | Sodium: 1,070mg | Fiber: 3g | Carbohydrates: 19g | Sugar: 2g

Caveman's Cabbage Soup

Slow cooking cabbage soup preserves the nutrients in the cabbage and other vegetables, while higher-temperature methods of preparation tend to destroy many of the nutrients.

INGREDIENTS | SERVES 14

1 small head of cabbage
2 green onions
1 red bell pepper
1 bunch celery
1 cup baby carrots
4 cups chicken broth
4 cups water
3 cloves garlic, minced
¼ teaspoon red pepper flakes
¼ teaspoon dried basil
¼ teaspoon dried oregano
¼ teaspoon dried thyme
¼ teaspoon onion powder

1. Chop all vegetables and place them in a 6-quart slow cooker.

2. Pour in the broth and water.

3. Stir in garlic, red pepper flakes, basil, oregano, thyme, and onion powder. Cover and cook on low for 8–10 hours.

PER SERVING: Calories: 49 | Fat: 1g | Protein: 2g | Sodium: 314mg | Fiber: 2g | Carbohydrates: 8g | Sugar: 3g

Pork and Apple Stew

If you prefer a tart apple taste, you can substitute Granny Smith apples for the Golden Delicious.
(You can also add more apples if you wish. Apples and pork were made for each other!)

INGREDIENTS | SERVES 8

1 (3-pound) boneless pork shoulder roast

Freshly ground black pepper, to taste

1 large sweet onion, peeled and diced

2 Golden Delicious apples, peeled, cored, and diced

1 (2-pound) bag baby carrots

2 stalks celery, finely diced

2 cups apple juice

¼ cup dry vermouth (optional)

2 tablespoons brandy (optional)

2 tablespoons honey (optional)

½ teaspoon dried thyme

¼ teaspoon ground allspice

¼ teaspoon dried sage

2 large sweet potatoes, peeled and quartered

Herb and Spice Test

If you're unsure about the herbs and spices suggested in a recipe, wait to add them until the end of the cooking time. Once the meat is cooked through, spoon out ¼ cup or so of the pan juices into a microwave-safe bowl. Add a pinch of each herb and spice (in proportion to how they're suggested in the recipe), microwave on high for 15–30 seconds, and then taste the broth to see if you like it. Season the dish accordingly.

1. Trim the roast of any fat; discard the fat and cut the roast into bite-sized pieces. Add the pork to a 4-quart slow cooker along with the remaining ingredients in the order given. Rest the sweet potato quarters on top of the mixture in the slow cooker.

2. Cover and cook on low for 6 hours or until the pork is cooked through and tender.

PER SERVING: Calories: 326 | Fat: 12g | Protein: 34g | Sodium: 226mg | Fiber: 4g | Carbohydrates: 18g | Sugar: 12g

Lamb Stew

This high-protein concoction is a guaranteed Paleo crowd-pleaser.

INGREDIENTS | SERVES 4

1½ pounds boneless lamb shoulder, fat trimmed

1 cup Beef Stock (page 79)

6 medium carrots, cut into ¾-inch pieces

12 ounces turnips, cut into ¾-inch pieces

¾ cup chopped onions

½ tablespoon crushed garlic

¼ teaspoon thyme

¼ teaspoon rosemary, crumbled

½ teaspoon freshly ground black pepper

1. Cut lamb into 1½" chunks.

2. Combine all the ingredients into a 4-quart slow cooker and cook on low for 8–10 hours.

3. Before serving, skim off and discard fat.

PER SERVING: Calories: 532 | Fat: 32g | Protein: 32g | Sodium: 227mg | Fiber: 7g | Carbohydrates: 29g | Sugar: 14g

Texas Firehouse Chili

This no-bean chili is similar to dishes entered into firehouse chili cookoffs all over Texas.

INGREDIENTS | SERVES 4

1 pound cubed lean beef

2 tablespoons onion powder

1 tablespoon garlic powder

2 tablespoons Mexican-style chili powder

1 tablespoon paprika

½ teaspoon oregano

½ teaspoon freshly ground black pepper

½ teaspoon white pepper

½ teaspoon cayenne pepper

½ teaspoon ground chipotle chile pepper

8 ounces tomato sauce

1. Quickly brown the beef for 5–7 minutes in a nonstick skillet. Drain off any excess grease.

2. Add the meat and all of the remaining ingredients to a 4-quart slow cooker. Cook on low for up to 10 hours.

PER SERVING: Calories: 212 | Fat: 8g | Protein: 26g | Sodium: 359mg | Fiber: 2.5g | Carbohydrates: 9g | Sugar: 3g

Simple Tomato Soup

*This simple, healthy, three-step soup is made with canned tomatoes,
which are available year-round at affordable prices. You can also make this soup
with about 4 pounds of chopped fresh tomatoes if you prefer.*

INGREDIENTS | SERVES 8

1 small sweet onion, finely diced

3 tablespoons coconut butter

3 (14½-ounce) cans diced tomatoes

1 tablespoon honey

15 ounces Chicken Stock (page 78)

½ teaspoon lemon juice

1. In a small glass or microwave-safe bowl, cook onions and coconut butter in the microwave on high for 1 minute to soften them.

2. Add onion mixture, tomatoes, honey, and chicken stock to a greased 4-quart slow cooker. Cook on high for 4 hours or on low for 8 hours.

3. Turn off slow cooker. Add lemon juice to the soup. Allow soup to cool for about 20 minutes, and then blend using an immersion blender or by pouring the soup in batches into a standard blender.

PER SERVING: Calories: 45 | Fat: 0g | Protein: 2g | Sodium: 223mg | Fiber: 2g | Carbohydrates: 10g | Sugar: 6g

Chapter 6

Beef, Pork, and Lamb

Tomato-Braised Pork

Here the pork is gently cooked in tomatoes to yield meltingly tender meat.
If you'd prefer oregano or thyme in place of the marjoram, consider using a bit
less than what the recipe calls for, as these herbs tend to have a stronger flavor.

INGREDIENTS | SERVES 4

1 (28-ounce) can crushed tomatoes

3 tablespoons tomato paste

1 cup loosely packed fresh basil

½ teaspoon freshly ground black pepper

½ teaspoon marjoram

1¼ pounds boneless pork roast

1. Place the tomatoes, tomato paste, basil, pepper, and marjoram into a 4-quart slow cooker. Stir to create a uniform sauce. Add the pork.

2. Cook on low for 7–8 hours or until the pork easily falls apart when poked with a fork.

PER SERVING: Calories: 192 | Fat: 5g | Protein: 32g | Sodium: 166mg | Fiber: 1g | Carbohydrates: 3g | Sugar: 2g

Honey-Mustard Pork Loin

A mixture of mustard and honey keeps the pork from drying out during the long cooking time.

INGREDIENTS | SERVES 2

3 tablespoons Dijon mustard

1 tablespoon mild honey

½ pound pork tenderloin

1. In a small bowl, mix the mustard and honey. Spread the mixture on the pork tenderloin in an even layer.

2. Place into a 2-quart slow cooker. Cook on low for 6 hours.

PER SERVING: Calories: 170 | Fat: 3g | Protein: 25g | Sodium: 326mg | Fiber: 1g | Carbohydrates: 10g | Sugar: 9g

Pork Tenderloin with Sweet and Savory Apples

The tart apples sweeten over the long cooking time and nearly melt into the pork.

INGREDIENTS | SERVES 2

¼ teaspoon freshly ground black pepper

¾–1 pound boneless pork tenderloin

½ cup sliced onions

5 fresh sage leaves

2 cups peeled, diced Granny Smith apples

Pork Tenderloin Tip

Lean, boneless pork tenderloin is often sold in very large packages containing two or more tenderloins, with a combined weight that is frequently over 15 pounds. As a result, it can be very expensive. Buy pork tenderloin on sale, and cut the meat into meal-sized portions. Label and freeze the portions until they are needed.

1. Sprinkle pepper on the tenderloin. Place the onion slices on the bottom of a 1½- to 2-quart slow cooker. Add the tenderloin. Place the sage on top of the meat. Top with the diced apples.

2. Cover and cook on low for 8–10 hours.

PER SERVING: Calories: 261 | Fat: 5g | Protein: 47g | Sodium: 120mg | Fiber: 1g | Carbohydrates: 4g | Sugar: 2g

Beef and Coconut Curry

This Indian-inspired recipe combines the perfect blend of beef and vegetables, and the finished product is both sweet and savory.

INGREDIENTS | SERVES 4

2 tablespoons canola oil

2 pounds beef chuck roast, cut into 2-inch pieces

2 large onions, cut into 8 wedges each

4 cloves garlic, finely chopped

2 tablespoons finely chopped fresh ginger

12 ounces coconut milk

2 tablespoons honey

1 tablespoon curry powder

1 teaspoon cayenne pepper

1 pint cherry tomatoes

1. In a large skillet, warm oil over medium-high heat. Brown beef on all sides. Transfer to a 4-quart slow cooker along with onions, garlic, and ginger.

2. In a large bowl, whisk together the coconut milk, honey, curry powder, and cayenne pepper, and pour over meat. Cover and cook on low until meat is fork tender, about 4–5 hours.

3. Stir in cherry tomatoes and let them warm and soften in stew for 15–20 minutes.

PER SERVING: Calories: 315 | Fat: 25g | Protein: 4g | Sodium: 20mg | Fiber: 3g | Carbohydrates: 23g | Sugar: 14g

Curried Buffalo

This recipe using buffalo meat is made to impress even the fussiest Paleo eaters.

INGREDIENTS | SERVES 4

3 tablespoons arrowroot powder

3 tablespoons curry powder

1½ pounds buffalo shoulder roast, cubed

3 large carrots, peeled and sliced

3 zucchini, sliced

2 medium butternut squash, peeled and cubed

2 teaspoons crushed garlic

1 cup Beef Stock (page 79)

1. Combine the arrowroot and curry powder in a zip-top plastic bag.

2. Add buffalo to bag and shake gently until meat is coated.

3. Put vegetables and garlic into a 4-quart slow cooker, and then add the seasoned meat.

4. Pour stock over the meat and vegetables in the slow cooker. Cover and cook for 8–9 hours on low or 4–5 hours on high.

PER SERVING: Calories: 132 | Fat: 1g | Protein: 4g | Sodium: 101mg | Fiber: 7g | Carbohydrates: 29g | Sugar: 11g

Beef and Cabbage

The longer cooking time helps the flavors develop. But because the meat in this recipe is already cooked, this meal is done when the cabbage is tender, or in about 4 hours on low heat. Serve over mashed turnip, cauliflower, or butternut squash.

INGREDIENTS | SERVES 4

1 pound cooked stew beef
1 small head of cabbage, chopped
1 medium onion, peeled and diced
2 large carrots, peeled and thinly sliced
2 stalks celery, sliced in ½-inch pieces
1 clove garlic, peeled and minced
2 cups beef broth
1 (14½-ounce) can diced tomatoes
¼ teaspoon honey
⅛ teaspoon freshly ground black pepper

1. Cut the cooked beef into bite-sized pieces and add it to a 4-quart slow cooker along with the cabbage, onion, carrots, and celery. Stir to combine.

2. Add the garlic, broth, tomatoes, honey, and pepper to a bowl; mix well and pour over the beef. Cook on high for 1 hour or until the cabbage has begun to wilt.

3. Reduce heat to low and cook for 3–4 hours or until cabbage is very tender. Adjust seasonings if necessary.

PER SERVING: Calories: 354 | Fat: 8g | Protein: 29g | Sodium: 241mg | Fiber: 12g | Carbohydrates: 43g | Sugar: 21g

Easy Leg of Lamb

Although lamb can be an expensive cut of meat, you can often find it on sale during the holidays. Stock up on several cuts and freeze them when you find good prices.

INGREDIENTS | SERVES 6

1 (4-pound) bone-in leg of lamb

5 cloves garlic, peeled and cut into spears

2 tablespoons olive oil

1 tablespoon dried rosemary

½ teaspoon freshly ground black pepper

4 cups Chicken Stock (page 78)

¼ cup red wine

1. Make small incisions evenly over the lamb. Place garlic spears into the slices in the lamb.

2. Rub olive oil, rosemary, and pepper over the lamb. Place lamb into a greased 4- to 6-quart slow cooker.

3. Pour stock and wine around the leg of lamb. Cook on high for 4 hours or on low for 8 hours.

4. Serve the roast lamb in bowls. Ladle the sauce from the slow cooker over each serving.

PER SERVING: Calories: 74 | Fat: 5g | Protein: 7g | Sodium: 15mg | Fiber: 1g | Carbohydrates: 3g | Sugar: 1g

Herbed Lamb Chops

This simple herb rub would make a fun holiday gift to give to friends or family members who enjoy cooking! Include this recipe with a small jar of the rub.

INGREDIENTS | SERVES 4

1 medium onion, sliced
1 teaspoon dried oregano
½ teaspoon dried thyme
½ teaspoon garlic powder
⅛ teaspoon freshly ground black pepper
2 pounds (about 8) lamb loin chops
1 tablespoon olive oil

1. Place the onion on the bottom of a greased 4-quart slow cooker.

2. In a small bowl, mix together oregano, thyme, garlic powder, and pepper. Rub herb mixture over the lamb chops.

3. Place herb-rubbed lamb chops over the sliced onions in the slow cooker. Drizzle olive oil over the lamb chops.

4. Cook on high for 3 hours or on low for 6 hours, until tender.

PER SERVING: Calories: 43 | Fat: 3g | Protein: 0g | Sodium: 2mg | Fiber: 1g | Carbohydrates: 3g | Sugar: 1g

Easy Slow-Cooker Pork Tenderloin

Slow-cooker meals are a great way to cook for your family. Large quantities can be thrown into the cooker hours in advance. Most leftovers can be easily frozen for future meals.

INGREDIENTS | SERVES 4

1 pound lean pork loin, whole

1 (28-ounce) can diced tomatoes, no salt added

3 medium zucchini, diced

4 cups cauliflower florets

Chopped fresh basil, to taste

Garlic, to taste

Low-Fat Meat Choice

Pork is a nice low-fat protein source. It is versatile for cooking and quite flavorful. This often-overlooked meat is a fantastic friend of the Paleolithic lifestyle.

1. Combine all the ingredients in a 2- or 4-quart slow cooker.

2. Cook on low for 6–7 hours.

PER SERVING: Calories: 58 | Fat: 1g | Protein: 3g | Sodium: 310mg | Fiber: 4g | Carbohydrates: 13g | Sugar: 6g

Paleo Pulled Pork

This recipe was inspired by an elite athlete, Allie, a field hockey goalie playing at the collegiate level. Allie often enjoys this pulled-pork recipe as her postgame celebratory meal.

INGREDIENTS | SERVES 8

2½ pounds pork loin

1 large onion, chopped

1 (16-ounce) can unsalted organic tomato paste

3 tablespoons olive oil

2 cups lemon juice

½ cup unsalted beef broth

4 cloves garlic

¼ teaspoon cayenne pepper

½ teaspoon paprika

2 teaspoons ground chipotle chile pepper

1 teaspoon thyme

1 teaspoon cumin

1. Combine all the ingredients in a 4- to 6-quart slow cooker.

2. Cook on low for 5 hours or until meat is softened completely.

3. Once cooled, shred with a fork and serve over a large dinner salad or a hot root vegetable medley.

PER SERVING: Calories: 116 | Fat: 6g | Protein: 3g | Sodium: 506mg | Fiber: 3g | Carbohydrates: 18g | Sugar: 9g

Apples-and-Onions Pork Chops

Try Sonya apples in this sweet and savory dish; they are crisp and sweet.

INGREDIENTS | SERVES 4

4 crisp, sweet apples, peeled and cut into wedges

2 large onions, sliced

4 thick-cut boneless pork chops (about 1 pound)

½ teaspoon cayenne pepper

½ teaspoon ground cinnamon

¼ teaspoon allspice

¼ teaspoon ground fennel

1. Place half of the apple wedges in the bottom of an oval 4-quart slow cooker. Add half of the sliced onions.

2. Top with a single layer of pork chops. Sprinkle with spices, and top with the remaining apples and onions.

3. Cook on low for 8 hours.

PER SERVING: Calories: 267 | Fat: 6g | Protein: 42g | Sodium: 94mg | Fiber: 2g | Carbohydrates: 7g | Sugar: 3g

Slow Cooking with Boneless Pork

Not only is there less waste associated with boneless pork chops or roasts, there is often less fat attached to the meat. Even without much fat, boneless pork is well suited to slow cooking. All of the moisture stays in the dish, ensuring tender pork.

Pot Roast with a Touch of Sweet

Serve this roast alongside a hearty portion of "Mashed" Cauliflower (page 199).

INGREDIENTS | SERVES 4

1 teaspoon freshly ground black pepper
1 teaspoon smoked paprika
1 teaspoon garlic powder
1 teaspoon onion powder
½ cup lime juice
½ cup tomato sauce
2 pounds beef chuck roast
1 large sweet onion, thickly sliced
1 teaspoon coconut or olive oil
½ cup water
2 tablespoons red wine (optional)

1. In a small bowl, combine the pepper, paprika, garlic powder, and onion powder.

2. In a separate bowl, combine the lime juice and tomato sauce. Set aside.

3. Season all sides of the roast with the prepared spice mixture.

4. Place onion slices on the bottom of a 4-quart slow cooker.

5. Warm the oil in a large skillet over medium-high heat. Brown the roast on all sides in the skillet.

6. Place browned roast on top of the onions in the slow cooker. Turn stovetop heat to low, and add water and wine to the skillet.

7. Pour pan liquid over the roast, then the lime juice and sauce mixture on top. Cover and cook on low for 8 hours.

PER SERVING: Calories: 36 | Fat: 0g | Protein: 1g | Sodium: 164mg | Fiber: 2g | Carbohydrates: 7g | Sugar: 3g

Beef and Ginger Curry

*This hearty and spicy curry dish, typically served over rice,
is just as tasty over a bed of Paleo-approved carrots and cauliflower.*

INGREDIENTS | SERVES 4

1 pound stewing steak

1 tablespoon olive oil

Freshly ground black pepper, to taste

2 cloves garlic, minced

1 teaspoon chopped fresh ginger

1 fresh green chili pepper, diced

1 tablespoon curry powder

1 (14-ounce) can stewed tomatoes, chopped

1 large onion, peeled and quartered

8–9 ounces Beef Stock (page 79)

1. In a frying pan, brown the steak in the olive oil for 5–10 minutes. Once browned, remove from pan, leaving juices. Season beef with pepper.

2. In the remaining juice from the steak, cook the garlic, ginger, and chili pepper in the frying pan for 2 minutes, stirring frequently.

3. Season with curry powder. Mix in the chopped tomatoes.

4. Place the onion on bottom of a 2- or 4-quart slow cooker, and layer with browned beef.

5. Add tomato mixture from pan to the slow cooker, and add the beef stock. Cover and cook on low for 6–8 hours.

PER SERVING: Calories: 82 | Fat: 4g | Protein: 2g | Sodium: 192mg | Fiber: 4g | Carbohydrates: 16g | Sugar: 5g

Roast Beef for Two

Couples deserve a good roast dinner just as much as larger families.
So enjoy this one without having to eat leftovers for a week.

INGREDIENTS | SERVES 2

½ teaspoon freshly ground black pepper

½ teaspoon fennel seeds

½ teaspoon crushed rosemary

½ teaspoon dried oregano

¾ pound bottom round roast, excess fat removed

¼ cup Caramelized Onions (page 185)

¼ cup Beef Stock (page 79)

1 clove garlic, sliced

1. In a small bowl, stir the pepper, fennel seeds, rosemary, and oregano. Rub it onto all sides of the roast. Refrigerate for 15 minutes.

2. Place the roast in a 2-quart slow cooker. Add the onions, stock, and garlic. Cook on low for 6 hours or on high for 3 hours. Remove roast and slice. Serve the slices topped with the onions. Discard any cooking juices.

PER SERVING: Calories: 266 | Fat: 11g | Protein: 38g | Sodium: 172mg | Fiber: 1g | Carbohydrates: 4g | Sugar: 1g

Ground Beef Ragout

"Ragout" is a term that generally refers to a slow-cooked stew with a variety of vegetables that can be made with or without meat. Ground beef is used in this version for a very economical main dish. Serve over spaghetti squash or mashed cauliflower.

INGREDIENTS | SERVES 4

1 pound ground beef
2 medium onions, finely chopped
1 large green pepper, seeds removed, diced
1 tablespoon olive oil
1 (14½-ounce) can Italian-style stewed tomatoes
3 medium carrots, cut into ½-inch slices
½ cup Beef Stock (page 79)
½ teaspoon freshly ground black pepper
1 medium zucchini, halved lengthwise and cut into ½-inch slices

Not a Fan of Zucchini?

Instead of using zucchini, use yellow squash, precooked sweet potatoes, parsnips, or even mushrooms. Use whatever vegetables you have on hand!

1. Brown ground beef in a skillet, discard grease, and spoon ground beef into a greased 4-quart slow cooker.

2. In the same skillet, sauté the onions and green pepper in olive oil for 8–12 minutes, until softened. Add onions and green pepper to slow cooker.

3. Add the tomatoes, carrots, stock, and pepper to the slow cooker. Stir to combine all the ingredients.

4. Cook on high for 4 hours or on low for 8 hours.

5. An hour prior to serving, stir in the zucchini and allow to cook for 10–20 minutes, until fork-tender.

PER SERVING: Calories: 308 | Fat: 15g | Protein: 25g | Sodium: 264mg | Fiber: 5g | Carbohydrates: 20g | Sugar: 10g

Lamb with Garlic, Lemon, and Rosemary

You can use the spice rub in this recipe as a marinade by applying it to the leg of lamb several hours (or up to one full day) before cooking. The red wine in this dish can be replaced with Chicken or Beef Stock (pages 78–79).

INGREDIENTS | SERVES 4

4 cloves garlic, crushed

1 tablespoon chopped fresh rosemary

1 tablespoon olive oil

1 teaspoon freshly ground black pepper

1 (3-pound) leg of lamb

1 large lemon, cut into ¼-inch slices

½ cup red wine

1. In a small bowl, mix together garlic, rosemary, olive oil, and pepper. Rub this mixture onto the leg of lamb.

2. Place a few lemon slices in the bottom of a greased 4-quart slow cooker. Place spice-rubbed lamb on top of lemon slices.

3. Add remaining lemon slices on top of lamb. Pour wine around the lamb.

4. Cook on low for 8–10 hours or on high for 4–6 hours.

PER SERVING: Calories: 763 | Fat: 52g | Protein: 62g | Sodium: 194mg | Fiber: 0g | Carbohydrates: 2g | Sugar: 0g

Pork Tenderloin with Nectarines

Pork combined with the flavor of ripe nectarines makes a lovely sweet and slightly tangy sauce. Serve sliced pork and sauce over steamed zucchini strips.

INGREDIENTS | SERVES 4

1¼ pounds pork tenderloin

1 tablespoon olive oil

4 ripe but firm nectarines, each cut into 4 wedges

2 tablespoons lemon juice

Freshly ground black pepper, to taste

1. Rub pork tenderloin with olive oil. Place in a greased 4-quart slow cooker.

2. Place nectarine wedges on top of and around the pork tenderloin. Drizzle lemon juice over the pork and fruit. Cook on high for 3–4 hours or on low for 6–8 hours, until pork is very tender.

3. Remove pork from slow cooker and slice before serving. If needed, add pepper to taste.

PER SERVING: Calories: 246 | Fat: 7g | Protein: 31g | Sodium: 76mg | Fiber: 2g | Carbohydrates: 15g | Sugar: 11g

Sirloin Dinner

Add a tossed salad and some mashed sweet potato or butternut squash,
and this recipe makes a complete meal.

INGREDIENTS | SERVES 8

1 (4-pound) beef sirloin tip roast

2 tablespoons extra-virgin olive oil

½ teaspoon freshly ground black pepper

1 teaspoon garlic powder

1 teaspoon onion powder

1 teaspoon ground cumin

1 teaspoon dried thyme leaves, crushed

½ teaspoon sweet paprika

2 turnips, peeled and cut into 2-inch pieces

2 parsnips, peeled and cut into 2-inch pieces

1 (1-pound) bag baby carrots

8 cloves garlic, peeled and cut in half lengthwise

2 large onions, peeled and sliced

½ cup dry red wine

1 cup beef broth

Freshly ground black pepper, to taste

Rare Sirloin Roast

If you prefer a rare roast, use a probe thermometer set to your preferred doneness setting. (Choose 130°F for rare.) You'll need to be close by so that you hear the thermometer alarm when it goes off. Remove the roast to a platter; cover and keep warm. Cover and continue to cook the vegetables if necessary.

1. To ensure the roast cooks evenly, tie it into an even form using butcher's twine. Rub the oil onto the meat.

2. In a small bowl, mix the pepper, garlic powder, onion powder, cumin, thyme, and paprika. Pat the seasoning mixture on all sides of the roast. Place the roast in the slow cooker.

3. Arrange the turnips, parsnips, and carrots around the roast. Evenly disperse the garlic around the vegetables. Arrange the onion slices over the vegetables. Pour the wine and broth into the slow cooker. Season with pepper to taste. Cover and cook on low for 8 hours.

4. Use a slotted spoon to remove the roast and vegetables to a serving platter; cover and keep warm. Let the roast rest for at least 10 minutes before carving. To serve, thinly slice the roast across the grain. Serve drizzled with some of the pan juices.

PER SERVING: Calories: 109 | Fat: 4g | Protein: 2g | Sodium: 75mg | Fiber: 3g | Carbohydrates: 14g | Sugar: 6g

Mango Pork Morsels

In this recipe, the mango provides natural sweetness and a tropical flair.
Plate and pierce each morsel with a toothpick.

INGREDIENTS | SERVES 10

1½ pounds lean pork loin, cubed

2 mangoes, cubed

3 cloves garlic, minced

1 jalapeño, minced

1 tablespoon salsa

¼ teaspoon freshly ground black pepper

2 teaspoons ground chipotle chile pepper

1 teaspoon New Mexican chili powder

½ teaspoon oregano

2 tablespoons freshly squeezed juice from an orange

2 tablespoons lime juice

1. Quickly brown the pork in a nonstick skillet. Add the pork and mango to a 4-quart slow cooker.

2. In a small bowl, whisk together the garlic, jalapeño, salsa, pepper, chipotle, chili powder, oregano, and the orange and lime juices. Pour over the mango and pork. Stir.

3. Cook on low for 6 hours; uncover and cook on high for 30 minutes. Stir before serving.

PER SERVING: Calories: 29 | Fat: 0g | Protein: 0g | Sodium: 11mg | Fiber: 1g | Carbohydrates: 8g | Sugar: 6g

How to Cut Up a Mango

Slice the mango vertically on either side of the large flat pit. Using the tip of a knife, cut vertical lines into the flesh without piercing the skin. Make horizontal lines in the flesh to form cubes. Use a spoon to scoop out the cubes. Repeat for the other side.

Cabbage Rollatini

Serve alongside or atop a bed of mixed greens, and enjoy as a "taco salad."

INGREDIENTS | SERVES 12

1 tablespoon coconut oil

½ medium onion, ground in food processor

4 cloves garlic, ground in food processor

1 teaspoon dried basil

1 teaspoon cumin

1 teaspoon dried oregano

½ head cauliflower, ground in food processor

2 pounds ground meat (lean beef, chicken, or turkey)

½ cup almond flour

1 egg

½ teaspoon garlic powder

1 head green cabbage, leaves separated and heated in microwave

26 ounces tomato sauce (jarred, or recipe from Chapter 4)

1. Heat oil in a large skillet over medium heat. Add the ground onion, garlic, basil, cumin, and oregano and sauté for 2–3 minutes. Remove from heat.

2. In a large bowl, place the cauliflower, meat, almond flour, egg, and garlic powder. Combine thoroughly with your hands or a large spoon. Add in sautéed onion mixture and mix well.

3. Line a 4-quart slow cooker with 2 large cabbage leaves.

4. Scoop ½–¾ cup of the meat filling onto the stem ends of the remaining cabbage leaves, and roll each leaf as tightly as possible.

5. Place rolls in slow cooker, seam-side down. Pour tomato sauce evenly over top of cabbage rolls.

6. Cook on high for 4 hours. Serve warm, and spoon sauce and drippings over the rolls.

PER SERVING: Calories: 192 | Fat: 8g | Protein: 20g | Sodium: 386mg | Fiber: 4g | Carbohydrates: 11g | Sugar: 6g

Lunch Casserole

A filling, high-protein entrée, loaded with fiber, B-vitamins, and iron.

INGREDIENTS | SERVES 6

1½ pounds lean ground beef

1 large onion, chopped

2 tablespoons canola oil

2 cloves garlic, minced

6 ounces sliced mushrooms

½ teaspoon nutmeg

1 (10-ounce) package frozen spinach, thawed and squeezed dry

3 tablespoons arrowroot powder

6 eggs, beaten

¾ cup coconut milk, scalded

1. In a large skillet over medium heat, lightly brown the beef and onions in the canola oil for 5–10 minutes.

2. Drain the excess fat and place meat mixture in a well-greased 2- to 4-quart slow cooker.

3. Stir the garlic, mushrooms, nutmeg, spinach, and arrowroot powder into the meat mixture in the slow cooker.

4. In a small bowl, beat the eggs and coconut milk together. Pour over meat mixture in the slow cooker. Stir well.

5. Cover and cook on low for 7–9 hours or until firm.

PER SERVING: Calories: 365 | Fat: 22g | Protein: 34g | Sodium: 185mg | Fiber: 2g | Carbohydrates: 10g | Sugar: 2g

Barbecue Meatballs

This tangy yet spicy meatball recipe goes well with some southern-inspired vegetables, or alone as a crowd-pleasing appetizer.

INGREDIENTS | SERVES 4

1½ cups chili sauce

1 cup Fig Jam (page 39), or grape jelly

2 teaspoons Dijon mustard

1 pound lean ground beef

1 egg

3 tablespoons arrowroot powder

½ teaspoon lemon juice

1. Preheat oven to 400°F.

2. Combine the chili sauce, jam, and mustard in a 2-quart slow cooker and stir well.

3. Cover and cook on high while preparing meatballs.

4. In a large mixing bowl, combine the remaining ingredients thoroughly. Shape into 20 medium-sized meatballs. Place meatballs on a broiler rack or in a baking pan and bake in oven for 15–20 minutes. Drain well.

5. Add meatballs to the sauce in slow cooker. Stir well to coat.

6. Cover and cook on low for 6–10 hours.

PER SERVING: Calories: 586 | Fat: 8g | Protein: 37g | Sodium: 1,496mg | Fiber: 8g | Carbohydrates: 102g | Sugar: 82g

Stuffed Cabbage

This is a wonderful dish to serve to guests. Although there is some preparation to do, you will have plenty of time to clean up before your guests arrive.

INGREDIENTS | SERVES 4

Water, as needed
1 large head cabbage
1 teaspoon canola or flaxseed oil
½ cup sliced onions
1 (28-ounce) can whole tomatoes in purée
½ cup minced onions
1 egg
½ tablespoon garlic powder
½ tablespoon paprika
1 pound 94% lean ground beef

1. Bring a large pot of water to boil.

2. Meanwhile, using a knife, make 4 or 5 cuts around the core of the cabbage and remove the core. Discard the core and 2 layers of the outer leaves. Peel off 6–8 large whole leaves. Place the leaves in a steamer basket and allow them to steam over the boiling water for 7 minutes.

3. Allow the leaves to cool enough to handle. Dice the remaining cabbage to equal ½ cup.

4. In a nonstick skillet, add canola or flaxseed oil. Add the sliced onions and diced cabbage, and sauté for about 5 minutes until the onions are soft. Add tomatoes. Break up tomatoes into small chunks using the back of a spoon. Simmer about 10–15 minutes. Ladle one-third of the sauce over the bottom of a 4-quart oval slow cooker.

5. Place the minced onions, egg, spices, and beef into a medium bowl. Stir to distribute all ingredients evenly.

6. Place a cabbage leaf with the open side up and the stem facing you on a clean work area. Add about ¼ cup filling to the leaf toward the stem. Fold the sides together, and then pull the top down and over the filling to form a packet. It should look like a burrito. Repeat until all the filling is gone.

7. Arrange the cabbage rolls, seam-side down, in a single layer in the slow cooker. Ladle about half of the remaining sauce over the rolls. Repeat with a second layer of cabbage rolls, and ladle the remaining sauce over the rolls. Cover and cook on low for up to 10 hours.

PER SERVING: Calories: 282 | Fat: 8g | Protein: 34g | Sodium: 150mg | Fiber: 7g | Carbohydrates: 18g | Sugar: 9g

Meatloaf-Stuffed Green Peppers

This recipe is slightly different from traditional stuffed pepper recipes because it doesn't contain rice or potatoes to supplement the meat mixture. This is a great main dish option for those following low-carbohydrate food plans.

INGREDIENTS | SERVES 4

¼ cup almond flour
¼ cup coconut milk
1 pound ground beef
½ teaspoon lemon juice
½ teaspoon freshly ground black pepper
1½ teaspoons dried onion
1 egg
4 green peppers
⅓ cup water

1. In a large bowl, mix together the almond flour and coconut milk, and set aside for 5 minutes.

2. Next, add the ground beef, lemon juice, pepper, dried onion, and egg to the mixture. Mix together well.

3. Carefully remove the tops, seeds, and membranes of the peppers. Fill each pepper with one-quarter of the meatloaf mixture.

4. Place the stuffed peppers in a greased 4-quart slow cooker. Add ⅓ cup of water around the bottom of the stuffed peppers.

5. Cook on high for 3–4 hours or on low for 6–8 hours, until green peppers are softened.

PER SERVING: Calories: 308 | Fat: 19g | Protein: 27g | Sodium: 97mg | Fiber: 3g | Carbohydrates: 8g | Sugar: 3g

Chapter 7

Poultry

Tuscan Chicken

This simple dish is perfect served over grilled or oven-roasted asparagus.

INGREDIENTS | SERVES 4

1 pound boneless, skinless chicken breast tenderloins

1 cup Chicken Stock (page 78)

4 cloves garlic, minced

1 shallot, minced

2 tablespoons lime juice

1 tablespoon lemon juice

1 tablespoon minced fresh rosemary

1. Place all the ingredients into a 4-quart slow cooker. Stir.

2. Cook on low for 4 hours or until the chicken is fully cooked.

PER SERVING: Calories: 141 | Fat: 3g | Protein: 25g | Sodium: 136mg | Fiber: 0g | Carbohydrates: 2g | Sugar: 0g

Coconut Mango Spiced Chicken

This simple, sweet, and spicy dish requires just four ingredients, and is easily prepared in just a few minutes.

INGREDIENTS | SERVES 4

1 can coconut milk

1 large (softball-size) firm mango, peeled and cut into cubes (save pit)

1 pound chicken breasts or thighs, cut into cubes

1 tablespoon dried paprika flakes

1. Pour coconut milk into a 4-quart slow cooker.

2. Place the cubes of mango into the slow cooker, along with the pit of the mango. Add the chicken and paprika flakes. Stir well.

3. Cook on high for 3 hours or on low for 5–6 hours.

PER SERVING: Calories: 133 | Fat: 3g | Protein: 24g | Sodium: 131mg | Fiber: 1g | Carbohydrates: 1g | Sugar: 0g

Chicken Cacciatore

This recipe can be prepared using a variety of different vegetable combinations as substitutes for the mushrooms and green peppers. For example, try sliced carrots, sliced zucchini and summer squash, eggplant, yellow or red pepper, etc.

INGREDIENTS | SERVES 6

6 skinless, boneless chicken breasts
21 ounces tomato sauce
9 ounces fresh mushrooms
2 green peppers, seeded and cubed
1 large onion, sliced
1–2 cloves garlic, minced

1. Place all ingredients in a 4-quart slow cooker. Cover and cook on low for 7–9 hours.

2. Serve warm over vegetable medley of choice.

PER SERVING: Calories: 319 | Fat: 7g | Protein: 53g | Sodium: 791mg | Fiber: 3g | Carbohydrates: 11g | Sugar: 7g

Pheasantly Pleasant

Wild game like pheasants move more frequently than the average chicken and therefore contain less saturated fat and calories per ounce.

INGREDIENTS | SERVES 6

2 pheasants, cut into 1- to 2-inch chunks
¼ cup almond flour, seasoned with freshly ground black pepper
4 tablespoons olive oil
4 tablespoons coconut butter
1 clove garlic
1 large onion, diced
1 cup sweet white wine
1 tablespoon honey
1 (10¾-ounce) can of chopped mushrooms
10 ounces chicken broth

1. Mix pheasant pieces in seasoned almond flour.

2. In a skillet over medium heat, sauté the pheasant for 5–7 minutes in oil and butter. Transfer pheasant to a 4-quart slow cooker.

3. Mash garlic clove in skillet juices, and add onion, wine, honey, mushrooms, and broth. Heat to bubbling and simmer 5 minutes, and pour over pheasant in the slow cooker.

4. Cover and cook on low for 6–8 hours.

PER SERVING: Calories: 493 | Fat: 21g | Protein: 58g | Sodium: 381mg | Fiber: 1g | Carbohydrates: 10g | Sugar: 5g

No-Crust Chicken Potpie

A traditional "comfort" food converted to satisfy even the hardest-to-please Paleo palate.

INGREDIENTS | SERVES 4

Butter-flavored cooking spray

10 ounces coconut milk

1 teaspoon dried parsley flakes

1 teaspoon dried onion flakes

1 (16-ounce) package frozen cauliflower, broccoli, and carrot blend

1 pound skinless, boneless chicken breasts, cut into ½-inch cubes

1. Spray a 4-quart slow cooker with butter-flavored cooking spray.

2. Combine coconut milk, parsley flakes, and onion flakes.

3. Stir in the frozen vegetables and chicken pieces. Cover and cook on low for 8 hours. Mix well before serving.

PER SERVING: Calories: 293 | Fat: 18g | Protein: 27g | Sodium: 166mg | Fiber: 3g | Carbohydrates: 7g | Sugar: 3g

Ground Turkey Joes

This easy sweet-and-sour turkey dish comes together quickly and serves well over puréed cauliflower, mashed sweet potatoes, or turnips. If you prefer, you can also use ground chicken or ground beef as a substitute for the ground turkey.

INGREDIENTS | SERVES 4

2 teaspoons olive oil

1 pound lean ground turkey

½ cup finely chopped onion

½ cup finely chopped green pepper

1 teaspoon garlic powder

1 tablespoon prepared yellow mustard

¾ cup Homemade Ketchup (page 73)

3 tablespoons honey

¼ teaspoon lemon juice

½ teaspoon freshly ground black pepper

1. In a large skillet, heat olive oil over medium-high heat. Brown ground turkey, onion, and green pepper for approximately 5–6 minutes. Drain off any grease.

2. Add turkey mixture to a greased 2½- or 4-quart slow cooker. Add garlic powder, mustard, ketchup, honey, lemon juice, and black pepper.

3. Mix ingredients together and cook on low for 4 hours or on high for 2 hours.

PER SERVING: Calories: 270 | Fat: 12g | Protein: 20g | Sodium: 108mg | Fiber: 1g | Carbohydrates: 22g | Sugar: 20g

Roast Chicken with Lemon and Artichokes

This is an elegant twist on a simple roast chicken. Marinated artichoke hearts add a hint of zest while fresh lemons give the dish a bright flavor reminiscent of summer.

INGREDIENTS | SERVES 4

Nonstick cooking spray
1 small onion, quartered
1 large carrot, sliced
1 large lemon
3 cloves garlic
1 (4-pound) whole chicken
½ teaspoon freshly ground black pepper
2 tablespoons olive oil
1 (6-ounce) jar marinated artichoke hearts

Make a Quick Lemon Sauce

Make a sauce using the liquids from the cooked chicken by straining them into a saucepan. Whisk in 2 tablespoons of almond flour and cook on low heat until thickened. The resulting sauce will have a fragrant aroma of lemon, artichokes, and garlic. Serve over green beans or asparagus, or alongside a salad.

1. Grease a large 6-quart slow cooker with nonstick cooking spray.

2. Place the onion and carrot in the slow cooker. Cut the lemon in half. Place half of the lemon, along with the garlic cloves, into the cavity of the chicken.

3. Cut the remainder of the lemon into 4–5 large slices.

4. Place the chicken on top of the onion and carrot slices. Place lemon slices on top of the chicken. Sprinkle pepper over the chicken. Drizzle olive oil over the chicken. Cook on low for 6–8 hours or on high for 3–4 hours.

5. An hour before serving, place artichoke hearts (discarding the oil) over the top of the chicken.

PER SERVING: Calories: 611 | Fat: 21g | Protein: 96g | Sodium: 359mg | Fiber: 1g | Carbohydrates: 4g | Sugar: 2g

Chicken Paprikash

If you prefer not to cook with wine, replace it with an equal amount of chicken broth.

INGREDIENTS | SERVES 8

1 tablespoon coconut butter

1 tablespoon extra-virgin olive oil

1 large yellow onion, peeled and diced

2 cloves garlic, peeled and minced

3 pounds boneless, skinless chicken thighs

¼ teaspoon freshly ground black pepper

2 tablespoons Hungarian paprika

½ cup Chicken Stock (page 78)

¼ cup dry white wine

2 cups (full-fat) coconut milk

A Thought on Thinning

If the resulting sauce for the chicken paprikash is too thin, add more coconut milk.

1. Add the coconut butter, oil, and onion to a microwave-safe bowl; cover and microwave on high for 1 minute. Stir, re-cover, and microwave on high for another minute or until the onions are transparent.

2. Stir in the garlic; cover and microwave on high for 30 seconds. Add contents of the bowl to a greased 4- to 6-quart slow cooker.

3. Cut the chicken thighs into bite-sized pieces. Add the chicken to the slow cooker.

4. Stir in the pepper, paprika, stock, and wine; cover and cook on low for 6 hours or on high for 3 hours.

5. Stir in the coconut milk; cover and continue to cook long enough to bring the coconut milk to the same temperature, about 30 minutes.

6. Sprinkle each serving with additional paprika if desired. Serve immediately.

PER SERVING: Calories: 343 | Fat: 20g | Protein: 35g | Sodium: 154mg | Fiber: 0g | Carbohydrates: 4g | Sugar: 1g

Curried Chicken in Coconut Milk

*Chicken broth base is available from Minor's (www.soupbase.com) or
Redi-Base (www.redibase.com), or you can use chicken bouillon concentrate.*

INGREDIENTS | SERVES 4

1 small onion, peeled and diced
2 cloves garlic, peeled and minced
1½ tablespoons curry powder
1 cup coconut milk
¾ teaspoon chicken broth base
8 chicken thighs, skin removed

1. Add the onion, garlic, curry powder, coconut milk, and broth base to a 4-quart slow cooker. Stir to mix.

2. Add the chicken thighs. Cover and cook on low for 6 hours.

3. Use a slotted spoon to remove the thighs to a serving bowl. Whisk to combine the sauce and pour over the chicken.

PER SERVING: Calories: 292 | Fat: 18g | Protein: 29g | Sodium: 128mg | Fiber: 1g | Carbohydrates: 5g | Sugar: 1g

Poached Chicken

*Use this moist, tender poached chicken in any recipe that calls for cooked chicken.
It is especially good in salads and sandwiches.*

INGREDIENTS | SERVES 8

4–5 pounds whole chicken or chicken parts
1 large carrot, peeled
1 stalk celery
1 medium onion, peeled and quartered
1 cup water

1. Place the chicken into an oval 6-quart slow cooker. Arrange the vegetables around the chicken. Add the water. Cook on low for 7–8 hours.

2. Remove the skin before eating.

PER SERVING: Calories: 310 | Fat: 8g | Protein: 54g | Sodium: 206mg | Fiber: 1g | Carbohydrates: 2g | Sugar: 1g

Tarragon Chicken

The tarragon infuses the chicken with flavor without added fat.

INGREDIENTS | SERVES 4

2 split chicken breasts

2 cups loosely packed fresh tarragon

1 medium onion, peeled and sliced

¼ teaspoon freshly ground black pepper

1. Place the chicken in a 4-quart slow cooker. Top with remaining ingredients. Cook on low for 7–8 hours.

2. Remove the chicken from the slow cooker. Peel off the skin and discard. Discard the tarragon and onion.

PER SERVING: Calories: 146 | Fat: 3g | Protein: 25g | Sodium: 138mg | Fiber: 1g | Carbohydrates: 3g | Sugar: 1g

Mango Duck Breast

Slow-cooked mangoes soften and create their own sauce in this easy duck dish.

INGREDIENTS | SERVES 4

2 boneless, skinless duck breasts

1 large mango, cubed

¼ cup duck stock or Chicken Stock (page 78)

1 tablespoon ginger juice

1 tablespoon minced hot pepper

1 tablespoon minced shallot

Place all ingredients into a 4-quart slow cooker. Cook on low for 4 hours.

PER SERVING: Calories: 412 | Fat: 18g | Protein: 55g | Sodium: 225mg | Fiber: 0g | Carbohydrates: 3g | Sugar: 0g

Thyme-Roasted Turkey Breast

Slow-cooked turkey is so moist there's no basting required!

INGREDIENTS | SERVES 10

2 large onions, thinly sliced

1 (6- to 7-pound) turkey breast or turkey half

½ cup minced thyme

½ tablespoon freshly ground black pepper

½ tablespoon dried parsley flakes

½ tablespoon celery flakes

½ tablespoon mustard seed

1. Arrange the onion slices in a thin layer on the bottom of a 6- to 7-quart slow cooker.

2. Make a small slit in the skin of the turkey and spread the thyme between the skin and meat. Smooth the skin back onto the turkey.

3. In a small bowl, stir the pepper, parsley, celery flakes, and mustard seed. Rub the spice mixture into the skin of the turkey.

4. Place the turkey in the slow cooker on top of the onion layer. Cook for 8 hours. Remove the skin and onions and discard them before serving the turkey.

PER SERVING: Calories: 341 | Fat: 2g | Protein: 72g | Sodium: 146mg | Fiber: 1g | Carbohydrates: 4g | Sugar: 1g

Foolproof Chicken

The simplest chicken recipe there is, leaving no excuse to arrive home to a fully cooked chicken dinner, for just about any occasion.

INGREDIENTS | SERVES 6

3 pounds boneless, skinless chicken
24 ounces tomato sauce

Place chicken in a 4-quart slow cooker and add sauce. Cover and cook on low for 8 hours or on high for 4–5 hours. Once cooked, shred the chicken with a fork and enjoy.

PER SERVING: Calories: 282 | Fat: 6g | Protein: 49g | Sodium: 845mg | Fiber: 2g | Carbohydrates: 6g | Sugar: 5g

Hot Chicken Buffalo Bites

Love buffalo wings? Then you will love these chicken bites even more; they are made with juicy chicken breasts so you won't have to worry about bones. They are super easy and much less messy!

INGREDIENTS | SERVES 6

3 large chicken breasts, cut into 2-inch strips
2 tablespoons almond flour
¼ cup melted coconut butter
3 cloves garlic, peeled and minced
⅓ cup Frank's Red Hot sauce

Fresh Garlic Versus Garlic Powder

In a pinch you can use 1½ teaspoons garlic powder in this recipe. The garlic flavor won't be quite as pungent and rich as it is when you use fresh garlic, but it will still be easy and enjoyable.

1. Place chicken pieces into a greased 2½-quart slow cooker.

2. In a saucepan, whisk together the almond flour and melted coconut butter for 2–3 minutes to toast the flour.

3. Slowly whisk in the garlic and Frank's Red Hot sauce. Pour sauce over chicken in the slow cooker.

4. Cover and cook on high for 3 hours or on low for 6 hours. Serve with celery and carrot sticks. If using a larger slow cooker, make sure to reduce cooking time by about half.

PER SERVING: Calories: 145 | Fat: 4g | Protein: 24g | Sodium: 461mg | Fiber: 0g | Carbohydrates: 1g | Sugar: 0g

Rotisserie-Style Chicken

Here is a delicious alternative to buying rotisserie chicken in your grocery store. This flavorful roast chicken is incredibly easy to make in your slow cooker. For a fast weeknight meal, cook the chicken overnight in the slow cooker and serve for dinner the next day.

INGREDIENTS | SERVES 6

1 (4-pound) whole chicken
2 teaspoons paprika
½ teaspoon onion powder
½ teaspoon dried thyme
½ teaspoon dried basil
½ teaspoon white pepper
½ teaspoon cayenne pepper
½ teaspoon freshly ground black pepper
½ teaspoon garlic powder
2 tablespoons olive oil

Gravy

If you would like to make a gravy to go with the chicken, follow these directions: After removing the cooked chicken, turn slow cooker on high. Whisk ⅓ cup of almond flour into the cooking juices. Add pepper to taste and cook for 10–15 minutes, whisking occasionally, until sauce has thickened. Spoon gravy over chicken.

1. Rinse the chicken in cold water and pat dry with a paper towel.

2. In a small bowl, mix together the paprika, onion powder, thyme, basil, white pepper, cayenne pepper, black pepper, and garlic powder.

3. Rub spice mixture over entire chicken. Rub part of the spice mixture underneath the skin, making sure to leave the skin intact.

4. Place the spice-rubbed chicken in a greased 6-quart slow cooker. Drizzle olive oil evenly over the chicken. Cook on high for 3–3½ hours or on low for 4–5 hours.

5. Remove chicken carefully from the slow cooker and place on a large plate or serving platter.

PER SERVING: Calories: 401 | Fat: 14g | Protein: 64g | Sodium: 231mg | Fiber: 1g | Carbohydrates: 1g | Sugar: 0g

Turkey in Onion Sauce

This is an African-inspired dish. Serve it over a mashed root vegetable or savory vegetable side dish of choice.

INGREDIENTS | SERVES 8

5 large onions, peeled and thinly sliced
4 cloves garlic, peeled and minced
¼ cup fresh lemon juice
¼ teaspoon cayenne pepper
4 turkey thighs, skin removed
Freshly ground black pepper, to taste

1. Add the onions, garlic, lemon juice, and cayenne pepper to a 4-quart slow cooker; stir to combine. Nestle the turkey thighs into the onion mixture. Cover and cook on low for 8 hours.

2. Remove the turkey thighs and allow to cool enough to remove the meat from the bone. Leave the cover off of the slow cooker and allow the onion mixture to continue to cook for about 20–30 minutes, until the liquid has totally evaporated. (You can raise the setting to high to speed things up if you wish. Just be sure to stir the mixture occasionally to prevent the onions from burning.)

3. Stir the turkey into the onion mixture. Taste for seasoning and add pepper if desired. For more heat, add additional cayenne pepper, too.

PER SERVING: Calories: 42 | Fat: 0g | Protein: 1g | Sodium: 6mg | Fiber: 2g | Carbohydrates: 10g | Sugar: 4g

Homemade Turkey Breast

*A versatile recipe for turkey that can be used to top a lunch or dinner salad,
or mixed with some avocado and chopped grapes for a tasty "turkey salad."*

INGREDIENTS | SERVES 12

4 pounds bone-in turkey breasts, skin removed

Freshly ground black pepper, to taste

1 large onion, finely chopped

4 tablespoons coconut butter

4 tablespoons olive oil

2 cups Turkey Stock (page 80)

1. Season turkey liberally with pepper (and other herbs and spices of choice) and place in a 4-quart slow cooker.

2. Add onion to the slow cooker and place some onion inside the rib cavity.

3. Add the coconut butter, oil, and stock. Cover and cook on low for 7–9 hours or on high for 4–6 hours. Internal temperature of the turkey should read at least 165°F before it is removed from the slow cooker.

PER SERVING: Calories: 212 | Fat: 5g | Protein: 37g | Sodium: 113mg | Fiber: 0g | Carbohydrates: 1g | Sugar: 1g

Slow-Cooker Southwestern Chicken Salad

Be creative and vary the vegetables in the recipe, or be bold and incorporate some hot chili peppers or jalapeños!

INGREDIENTS | SERVES 4

16 ounces Slow-Cooked Salsa (page 42)
1 teaspoon freshly ground black pepper
1 teaspoon cumin
1 teaspoon chili powder
1 large onion, peeled, halved, and sliced
1 cup frozen sliced bell peppers
4 boneless, skinless chicken breasts
1 (14½-ounce) can diced tomatoes
Mixed salad greens
Avocado slices, for garnish

1. In a medium bowl, combine the salsa with the pepper, cumin, and chili powder.

2. Place the onion and peppers on the bottom of a 4-quart slow cooker.

3. Place the chicken breasts on top of the onion and peppers. Cover the chicken with the salsa and tomatoes. Cook on low for 8 hours.

4. Shred the chicken with a fork inside the slow cooker, and stir everything together to combine.

5. Serve over mixed salad greens garnished with avocado slices.

PER SERVING: Calories: 331 | Fat: 7g | Protein: 53g | Sodium: 540mg | Fiber: 2g | Carbohydrates: 10g | Sugar: 5g

Fall-Off-the-Bone Chicken

This rich French dish can stand on its own when served with just a tossed salad.

INGREDIENTS | SERVES 4

½ cup plus 2 tablespoons almond flour
8 bone-in chicken thighs, skin removed
2 tablespoons coconut butter
2 tablespoons olive oil
1 medium yellow onion, peeled and diced
1 cup dry white wine
1 cup chicken broth
½–1 teaspoon dried tarragon
1 cup (full-fat) coconut milk

Tarragon Chicken Cooking Times

After 3 hours on high, the chicken will be cooked through and ready to eat. Yet, if you prefer to leave the chicken cooking for a longer period, after 7–8 hours on low, the meat will be tender enough to fall away from the bone. You can then remove the bones before you stir in the coconut milk.

1. Add ½ cup flour and the chicken thighs to a gallon-sized plastic bag; close and shake to coat the chicken.

2. Add the coconut butter and oil to a large sauté pan and heat over medium-high heat. Add the chicken thighs; brown the chicken by cooking the pieces on one side for 5 minutes, and then turning them over and frying them for another 5 minutes. Drain the chicken on paper towels and then place in a 4- to 6-quart slow cooker. Cover the slow cooker. Set temperature to low.

3. Add the onion to the sauté pan; sauté until the onion is transparent, about 3–5 minutes. Stir in the remaining almond flour, cooking until the onion just begins to brown.

4. Slowly pour the wine into the pan, stirring to scrape the browned bits off of the bottom of the pan and into the sauce. Add the broth. Cook and stir for 15 minutes or until the sauce is thickened enough to coat the back of a spoon.

5. Stir the tarragon into the sauce, and then pour the sauce over the chicken in the slow cooker. Cover and cook on high for 3 hours or on low for 6 hours.

6. Pour the coconut milk into the slow cooker; cover and cook for an additional 15 minutes or until the milk is heated through. Test for seasoning and add additional spices and tarragon if needed. Serve immediately.

PER SERVING: Calories: 355 | Fat: 29g | Protein: 6g | Sodium: 273mg | Fiber: 2g | Carbohydrates: 12g | Sugar: 2g

Chicken and Artichokes

This is a dish that is great served with just a tossed salad to make it a complete meal.

INGREDIENTS | SERVES 4

8 boneless, skinless chicken thighs

½ cup Chicken Stock (page 78)

1 tablespoon fresh lemon juice

2 teaspoons dried thyme

1 clove garlic, peeled and minced

¼ teaspoon freshly ground black pepper

1 (13-ounce) can artichoke hearts, drained

Artichoke Hearts

You can use thawed frozen artichoke hearts in place of canned ones. Or, if all you have on hand are marinated artichoke hearts, drain them and add them to the recipe; simply omit the thyme and garlic if you do.

Add all the ingredients to the slow cooker; stir to mix. Cover and cook on low for 6 hours. If necessary, uncover and allow to cook for 30 minutes or more to thicken the sauce.

PER SERVING: Calories: 172 | Fat: 6g | Protein: 27g | Sodium: 123mg | Fiber: 0g | Carbohydrates: 1g | Sugar: 0g

Honey-Glazed Turkey

*If the turkey legs are large, you can remove the meat from the bone
before serving and increase the number of servings to six or eight.*

INGREDIENTS | SERVES 4

Nonstick cooking spray

¼ cup Apricot Butter (page 38)

2 tablespoons honey

1 tablespoon fresh lemon juice

1 tablespoon Fruity Balsamic Barbecue
  Sauce (page 60)

1 teaspoon paprika

1 teaspoon lime juice

¼ teaspoon freshly ground black pepper

½ teaspoon dried rosemary

½ teaspoon dried thyme

4 turkey legs, skin removed

1 teaspoon arrowroot powder

1 teaspoon cold water

Turkey Salad

Complete Step 1 through Step 3 of the
Honey-Glazed Turkey recipe. Remove the
turkey legs and allow to cool enough to
remove the meat from the bones while you
make the arrowroot slurry. Once the glaze
is thickened, stir in the turkey meat. Serve
on a bed of mixed greens.

1. Grease the insert of the slow cooker with nonstick spray. Turn the heat setting to high. Add the apricot butter, honey, lemon juice, and barbecue sauce. Once the mixture has heated enough to melt the apricot butter and honey into the mixture, stir in the paprika, lime juice, pepper, rosemary, and thyme.

2. Add the turkey legs, spooning the sauce over them. Cover, reduce the heat setting to low, and cook for 8 hours. Uncover, increase heat setting to high, and cook for ½ hour to reduce the pan juices.

3. Remove the turkey legs to a serving platter; cover and keep warm.

4. Combine the arrowroot powder and water in a small bowl; stir to mix, and then thin with a little of the pan juices. Stir the resulting arrowroot powder slurry into the slow cooker. Cook and stir for 5 minutes or until thickened enough to coat the back of a spoon. Pour the glaze over the turkey legs and serve.

PER SERVING: Calories: 144 | Fat: 0g | Protein: 0g | Sodium: 4mg |
Fiber: 1g | Carbohydrates: 13g | Sugar: 12g

Turkey Meatloaf

Instead of making the meatloaf entirely from ground turkey, you can use a combination of ground beef, ground pork, and ground turkey.

INGREDIENTS | SERVES 6

2 pounds ground turkey

1 large yellow onion, peeled and diced

2 stalks celery, finely diced

1 green bell pepper, seeded and diced

2 cloves garlic, peeled and minced

2 large eggs

1 cup arrowroot powder

2 teaspoons lemon juice

Freshly ground black pepper, to taste

½ cup Homemade Ketchup (page 73)

1 tablespoon honey

Chili powder, to taste (optional)

Slow Cooker Liner

Instead of placing two pieces of heavy-duty aluminum foil across each other and over the sides of the slow cooker, you can instead line it with a Reynolds Slow Cooker Liner (*www.reynoldspkg.com*) and then place the nonstick foil piece inside the liner.

1. Add the ground turkey, onion, celery, bell pepper, garlic, eggs, arrowroot powder, lemon juice, and black pepper to a large bowl; mix well with your hands. Form into a loaf to fit the size (round or oval) of your slow cooker.

2. Line the slow cooker with two pieces of heavy-duty aluminum foil long enough to reach up both sides of the slow cooker and over the edge, crossing one piece over the other. Place a piece of nonstick foil the size of the bottom of the slow cooker insert inside the crossed pieces of foil to form a platform for the meatloaf. (This is to make it easier to lift the meatloaf out of the slow cooker.)

3. Put the meatloaf on top of the nonstick foil. Spread the ketchup over the top of the meatloaf. Drizzle the honey and sprinkle the chili powder, if using, over the top of the ketchup. Cover and cook on low for 7 hours or until the internal temperature of the meatloaf registers 165°F.

4. Lift the meatloaf out of the slow cooker and place it on a cooling rack. Allow it to rest for 20 minutes before transferring it to a serving platter and slicing it.

PER SERVING: Calories: 377 | Fat: 14g | Protein: 29g | Sodium: 177mg | Fiber: 2g | Carbohydrates: 33g | Sugar: 12g

Cajun Chicken and Shrimp Creole

This light and savory surf-and-turf dish is jam-packed with flavor from a variety of fresh herbs and spices. It makes the perfect lunch-time portion.

INGREDIENTS | SERVES 6

1 pound boneless, skinless chicken thighs

1 red bell pepper, chopped

1 large onion, chopped

1 stalk celery, diced

1 (15-ounce) can stewed tomatoes, undrained and chopped

1 clove garlic, minced

1 tablespoon honey

2 teaspoons freshly ground black pepper

1¼ teaspoons dried oregano

1¼ teaspoons dried thyme

1 teaspoon paprika

1 teaspoon garlic powder

1 teaspoon cayenne pepper

1 pound large or jumbo shrimp, peeled and deveined

1 tablespoon lemon juice

1 teaspoon lime juice

1. Place chicken in a 4½-quart slow cooker, along with all other ingredients except the shrimp and citrus juices.

2. Cover and cook on low for 7–9 hours or on high for 3–4 hours.

3. Add shrimp and lemon and lime juices, cover, and cook on low for 45–60 minutes.

PER SERVING: Calories: 216 | Fat: 5g | Protein: 31g | Sodium: 284mg | Fiber: 3g | Carbohydrates: 12g | Sugar: 7g

Chapter 8

Fish and Seafood

Shrimp Fra Diavolo

Serve this spicy sauce over hot Paleo "Pasta" (page 178), i.e., spaghetti squash. Spaghetti squash is an excellent substitute for pasta. When cooked in the oven for 40–50 minutes, the squash becomes soft enough to lightly separate with a fork, forming an angel hair–like "pasta!"

INGREDIENTS | SERVES 4

1 teaspoon olive oil

1 medium onion, diced

3 cloves garlic, minced

1 teaspoon red pepper flakes

1 (15-ounce) can diced fire-roasted tomatoes

1 tablespoon minced Italian parsley

½ teaspoon freshly ground black pepper

¾ pound medium shrimp, peeled

Slow Cooking with Shrimp

When slow cooking with shrimp, resist the temptation to put the shrimp in at the beginning of the recipe. While it takes longer to overcook foods in the slow cooker, delicate shrimp can go from tender to rubbery very quickly. For most recipes, 20 minutes on high is sufficient cooking time for shrimp.

1. Heat the oil in a nonstick skillet. Sauté the onion, garlic, and red pepper flakes for 8–10 minutes, until the onion is soft and translucent.

2. Add the onion mixture, tomatoes, parsley, and black pepper to a 4-quart slow cooker. Stir. Cook on low for 2–3 hours.

3. Add the shrimp. Stir, cover, and cook on high for 15 minutes or until the shrimp is fully cooked.

PER SERVING: Calories: 116 | Fat: 3g | Protein: 18g | Sodium: 127mg | Fiber: 1g | Carbohydrates: 5g | Sugar: 1g

Ginger-Lime Salmon

The slow cooker does all the work in this recipe, creating a healthy yet impressive dish that requires virtually no hands-on time.

INGREDIENTS | SERVES 12

1 (3-pound) salmon fillet, bones removed

¼ cup minced fresh ginger

¼ cup lime juice

1 lime, thinly sliced

1 large onion, peeled and thinly sliced

Cracked!

Before each use, check your slow cooker for cracks. Even small cracks in the glaze can allow bacteria to grow in the ceramic insert. If there are cracks, replace the insert or the whole slow cooker.

1. Place the salmon skin-side down in an oval 6–7-quart slow cooker. Pour the ginger and lime juice over the fish. Arrange the lime slices and then the onion slices in single layers over the fish.

2. Cook on low for 3–4 hours or until the fish is fully cooked and flaky. Remove the skin before serving.

PER SERVING: Calories: 166 | Fat: 7g | Protein: 22g | Sodium: 50mg | Fiber: 0g | Carbohydrates: 2g | Sugar: 1g

Salmon with Lemon, Capers, and Rosemary

Salmon is amazingly moist and tender when cooked in the slow cooker.

INGREDIENTS | SERVES 2

8 ounces salmon

⅓ cup water

2 tablespoons lemon juice

3 thin slices fresh lemon

1 tablespoon nonpareil capers

½ teaspoon minced fresh rosemary

1. Place the salmon on the bottom of a 2-quart slow cooker. Pour the water and lemon juice over the fish.

2. Arrange the lemon slices in a single layer on top of the fish. Sprinkle with capers and rosemary.

3. Cook on low for 2 hours. Discard lemon slices prior to serving.

PER SERVING: Calories: 165 | Fat: 7g | Protein: 22g | Sodium: 54mg | Fiber: 0g | Carbohydrates: 2g | Sugar: 1g

Romaine-Wrapped Halibut Steaks

Enjoy this very healthy, lean seafood dish that is so tender it'll flake with just a light touch of a fork.

INGREDIENTS | SERVES 4

1 cup Chicken or Turkey Stock (page 78 or 80)

10–14 large romaine leaves

4 (4-ounce) halibut fillets

1 teaspoon bouquet garni or dried tarragon leaves

Freshly ground black pepper, to taste

½ cup fresh spinach, thinly sliced

Bouquet garni

A classic herb mixture frequently used for flavoring in meat and vegetable dishes. The herbs are typically tied together with cheesecloth, and removed before consumption. The herbs traditionally used include dried parsley, thyme, bay leaf, and sage.

1. Pour stock into a 4-quart slow cooker. Cover and cook on high for 20 minutes.

2. Immerse romaine leaves (removing center stem) in boiling water for about 30 seconds, until wilted. Drain leaves.

3. Sprinkle halibut with herbs, pepper, and spinach. Wrap each fillet in 2–4 romaine leaves and place seam-side down in slow cooker.

4. Cover and cook on high for 1 hour, or until the fish is tender and can be flaked with a fork.

PER SERVING: Calories: 132 | Fat: 3g | Protein: 24g | Sodium: 69mg | Fiber: 0g | Carbohydrates: 1g | Sugar: 0g

Foiled Fish Fillets

A simple low-cal, high-protein dish that is ready in just 2 hours.

INGREDIENTS | SERVES 2

2 firm white fish fillets (e.g., tilapia)
1 small fennel bulb, thinly sliced
1 tomato, thinly sliced
1 red onion, sliced into rings
1 teaspoon dried dill
Juice of 1 lime
Freshly ground black pepper, to taste

1. Place fish fillets on aluminum foil and top with fennel, tomato, and onion.

2. Sprinkle on dill and lime juice. Fold the foil over and connect the edges, making a packet.

3. Place the packets into a 6-quart slow cooker. Cover and cook on high for 2 hours. Season to taste with pepper.

PER SERVING: Calories: 159 | Fat: 1g | Protein: 26g | Sodium: 83mg | Fiber: 3g | Carbohydrates: 11g | Sugar: 5g

Caveman's Catfish

First time trying catfish? This recipe is easily spruced up with the addition of a few flavorful veggies (i.e.: tomatoes, onions, peppers, spinach, etc.).

INGREDIENTS | SERVES 4

4 catfish fillets
½ teaspoon dried dill
½ teaspoon dried basil
½ teaspoon dried thyme
2 lemons (1 juiced, 1 sliced into rings)

1. Place fish fillets on aluminum foil, sprinkle with herbs, and squeeze the juice of 1 lemon over fish.

2. Place the lemon slices on the fish, and fold the foil over and connect the edges, making a packet.

3. Place the packets into a 6-quart slow cooker. Cover and cook on high for 2 hours.

PER SERVING: Calories: 160 | Fat: 5g | Protein: 26g | Sodium: 69mg | Fiber: 1g | Carbohydrates: 3g | Sugar: 1g

Orange Tilapia

A sweet taste of the sea. Serve with a medley of colorful summer vegetables.

INGREDIENTS | SERVES 4

4 tilapia fillets

2 tablespoons lime juice

1 tablespoon honey

1 (10-ounce) can of mandarin oranges, drained

Freshly ground black pepper, to taste

1. Place fish fillets on aluminum foil, drizzle with lime juice and honey, and pour on the drained oranges.

2. Fold the foil over the fish and connect the edges, making a packet. Place the packets into a 6-quart slow cooker.

3. Cover and cook on high for 2 hours. Add pepper to taste.

PER SERVING: Calories: 194 | Fat: 5g | Protein: 27g | Sodium: 72mg | Fiber: 1g | Carbohydrates: 11g | Sugar: 10g

Mahi-Mahi and Green Vegetable Medley

A super-healthy (and simply prepared) meal, packed with fiber, protein, iron, omega-3s, B-vitamins, and phytonutrients.

INGREDIENTS | SERVES 2

8 asparagus stalks
2 cups broccoli florets
2 cups fresh spinach
1 tablespoon olive oil
¼ teaspoon freshly ground black pepper
½ teaspoon red pepper flakes
¼ cup lemon juice, divided
1 pound mahi-mahi

1. Place the vegetables in a 6-quart slow cooker.

2. In a separate bowl, combine the olive oil, pepper, red pepper flakes, and 1 tablespoon of lemon juice. Brush mixture on both sides of the mahi-mahi, and place fish on top of vegetables in the slow cooker.

3. Add remaining lemon juice. Cover and cook on low for 2–3 hours. The fish should flake easily with a fork.

PER SERVING: Calories: 296 | Fat: 9g | Protein: 45g | Sodium: 258mg | Fiber: 3g | Carbohydrates: 10g | Sugar: 2g

Shrimp Creole

This Big Easy–inspired recipe may also be made by substituting meat or another seafood for the shrimp.

INGREDIENTS | SERVES 2

1 (8-ounce) can tomato sauce

1 (28-ounce) can whole tomatoes, broken up

1½ cups diced celery

1¼ cups chopped onion

1 cup chopped bell pepper

1 clove garlic, minced

¼ teaspoon pepper

6 drops Tabasco sauce, or to taste

1 pound medium shrimp, peeled and deveined

1. Combine all the ingredients except shrimp in a 4-quart slow cooker. Cook on high for 3–4 hours or on low for 6–8 hours.

2. Add shrimp during last hour of cooking, or during final 20 minutes if cooking on high. Serve over hot veggies.

PER SERVING: Calories: 337 | Fat: 4g | Protein: 49g | Sodium: 998mg | Fiber: 6g | Carbohydrates: 24g | Sugar: 12g

Herbed Tilapia Stew

Any type of white fish fillets (such as haddock or cod) will also work in this recipe. Fish cooks very, very quickly even on the low setting in a slow cooker, so this is one recipe you will need to set a timer for.

INGREDIENTS | SERVES 6

Nonstick cooking spray

2 pounds frozen boneless tilapia fillets

4 tablespoons canola oil

1 (14½-ounce) can diced tomatoes, with juice

4 cloves garlic, minced

½ cup sliced green onions

2 teaspoons Thai fish sauce

2 tablespoons fresh thyme, chopped, or 1 teaspoon dried thyme

1. Grease a 4-quart slow cooker with nonstick cooking spray. Place all the ingredients in the slow cooker.

2. Cover and cook on high for 1½–2 hours or on low for 2½–3 hours. Watch the cooking time. If your fish fillets are very thin, you may need to reduce the cooking time.

3. When fish is cooked through, fillets will easily separate and flake with a fork. Break the fish up into the tomatoes and cooking liquids.

PER SERVING: Calories: 87 | Fat: 9g | Protein: 0g | Sodium: 2mg | Fiber: 0g | Carbohydrates: 1g | Sugar: 0g

Scallop and Shrimp Jambalaya

This version of a "red" jambalaya originated in the French Quarter of New Orleans when saffron wasn't readily available. This Creole-type jambalaya contains tomatoes, whereas a rural Cajun jambalaya (also known as "brown jambalaya") does not.

INGREDIENTS | SERVES 8

2 tablespoons olive oil

1 large onion, chopped

2 medium stalks celery, chopped

1 medium green bell pepper, chopped

3 cloves garlic, minced

1 (28-ounce) can diced tomatoes, with juice

1 tablespoon dried parsley flakes

½ teaspoon dried thyme

½ teaspoon salt

¼ teaspoon freshly ground black pepper

¼ teaspoon red pepper sauce

2 teaspoons gluten-free Creole seasoning

¾ pound uncooked frozen scallops, thawed

¾ pound uncooked medium shrimp, peeled, deveined, and thawed if frozen

¼ cup fresh parsley, chopped

1. In a large skillet, heat the oil over medium heat. Sauté the onion, celery, and bell pepper until softened, about 3–5 minutes. Add garlic and cook for 1 minute more.

2. Grease a 4-quart slow cooker and add sautéed vegetables and all the remaining ingredients except the shrimp and parsley.

3. Cover and cook on low for 6 hours or on high for 3 hours.

4. Add shrimp and continue to cook on low for 45–60 minutes, or until shrimp are bright pink. Serve jambalaya over a root vegetable medley and garnish with chopped fresh parsley.

PER SERVING: Calories: 103 | Fat: 4g | Protein: 10g | Sodium: 204mg | Fiber: 2g | Carbohydrates: 7g | Sugar: 4g

Mix It Up

Use your favorite type of seafood instead of shrimp or scallops. Try a combination of scallops, cod, or diced tilapia, halibut, mahi-mahi, etc.

Fish "Bake"

The stewed tomatoes help prevent the fish from overcooking and make a sauce perfect for serving the fish over steamed cabbage, or alongside a vegetable dish of your choice.

INGREDIENTS | SERVES 4

2 tablespoons olive oil
4 flounder or cod fillets
1 clove garlic, peeled and minced
1 small onion, peeled and thinly sliced
1 green bell pepper, seeded and diced
1 (14½-ounce) can stewed tomatoes
½ teaspoon dried basil
½ teaspoon dried oregano
1 teaspoon dried parsley
Freshly ground black pepper, to taste

1. Add the oil to a 2- or 4-quart slow cooker. Use the oil to coat the bottom and the sides of the insert.

2. Rinse the fish fillets and pat dry with paper towels. Add to the slow cooker in a single layer over the oil.

3. Evenly distribute the garlic, onion, and bell pepper over the fish. Pour the stewed tomatoes over the fish. Evenly sprinkle the basil, oregano, parsley, and pepper over the tomatoes.

4. Cover and cook on low for 6 hours or until the fish is opaque and flakes apart.

PER SERVING: Calories: 223 | Fat: 8g | Protein: 31g | Sodium: 134mg | Fiber: 1g | Carbohydrates: 3g | Sugar: 1g

Cioppino

Inspired by Erin, the natural-born chef, whose specialty is low glycemic index–based cuisine.

INGREDIENTS | SERVES 6

2 tablespoons olive oil

1 large sweet onion, peeled and diced

2 stalks celery, finely diced

2 cloves garlic, peeled and minced

3 cups bottled clam juice or fish stock

2 cups water

1 (28-ounce) can diced or peeled Italian tomatoes

1 cup Zinfandel or other dry red wine

2 teaspoons dried parsley

1 teaspoon dried basil

1 teaspoon dried thyme

Red pepper flakes, to taste

1 teaspoon honey

1 bay leaf

1 pound cod, cut into 1-inch pieces

½ pound medium or large raw shrimp, peeled and deveined

½ pound scallops

1. Add the oil, onion, celery, and garlic to a 4-quart slow cooker. Stir to mix the vegetables together with the oil. Cover and cook on high for 30 minutes or until the onions are transparent.

2. Add the clam juice or fish stock, water, tomatoes, wine, parsley, basil, thyme, red pepper flakes, honey, and bay leaf. Stir to combine. Cover, reduce the heat setting to low, and cook for 5 hours.

3. If you used whole peeled tomatoes, use a spoon to break them apart. Gently stir in the cod, shrimp, and scallops. Increase the heat setting to high. Cover and cook for 30 minutes or until the seafood is cooked through. Ladle into soup bowls and serve immediately.

PER SERVING: Calories: 232 | Fat: 6g | Protein: 29g | Sodium: 168mg | Fiber: 1g | Carbohydrates: 6g | Sugar: 3g

Almond-Stuffed Flounder

Making this dish in the slow cooker lets you layer the fish and stuffing rather than stuffing and rolling the fillets. You can substitute sole for the flounder. Serve with a tossed salad and a seasoned vegetable medley of choice.

INGREDIENTS | SERVES 4

Nonstick cooking spray

4 (4-ounce) fresh or frozen flounder fillets

½ cup slivered almonds

1 tablespoon freeze-dried chives (optional)

Sweet paprika, to taste

¼ cup dry white wine (optional)

1 tablespoon coconut oil

½ cup grated carrot

1 tablespoon almond flour

¼ teaspoon dried tarragon

White pepper, to taste

1 cup (full-fat) coconut milk

1. Grease the insert of a 2- or 4-quart slow cooker with nonstick cooking spray.

2. Rinse the fish and pat dry with paper towels. Lay 2 fillets flat in the slow cooker. Sprinkle the almonds and chives (if using) over the fillets. Place the remaining fillets on top. Sprinkle paprika over the fish fillets. Pour the wine around the fish.

3. Add the oil and carrots to a microwave-safe bowl. Cover and microwave on high for 1 minute; stir and microwave on high for 1 more minute. Stir in the flour, tarragon, and pepper. Whisk in half the milk. Cover and microwave on high for 1 minute. Stir in the remaining milk. Pour the sauce over the fish.

4. Cover and cook on low for 2 hours or until the fish is cooked through and the sauce is thickened.

5. Turn off the slow cooker and let rest for 15 minutes. To serve, use a knife to cut through all layers into four wedges. Spoon each wedge onto a plate (so that there is fish and filling in each serving). Sprinkle with additional paprika before serving if desired.

PER SERVING: Calories: 309 | Fat: 20g | Protein: 25g | Sodium: 108mg | Fiber: 2g | Carbohydrates: 6g | Sugar: 1g

Poached Swordfish with Lemon-Parsley Sauce

Swordfish steaks are usually cut thicker than most fish fillets, plus they're a firmer fish so it takes longer to poach them. You can speed up the poaching process a little if you remove the steaks from the refrigerator and put them in room-temperature water during the 30 minutes that the onions and water are cooking.

INGREDIENTS | SERVES 4

1 tablespoon coconut butter

4 thin slices sweet onion

2 cups water

4 (6-ounce) swordfish steaks

1 lemon

2 tablespoons extra-virgin olive oil

2 teaspoons fresh lemon juice

¼ teaspoon Dijon mustard

Freshly ground white or black pepper, to taste (optional)

1 tablespoon fresh flat-leaf parsley, minced

Swordfish Salad

Triple the amount of lemon-parsley sauce and toss two-thirds of it together with 8 cups of salad greens. Arrange 2 cups of greens on each serving plate. Place a hot or chilled swordfish steak over each plate of the dressed greens. Spoon the additional sauce over the fish.

1. Use the coconut butter to grease the bottom and halfway up the sides of a 4-quart slow cooker.

2. Arrange the onion slices over the bottom of the slow cooker, pressing them into the butter so that they stay in place. Pour in the water. Cover and cook on high for 30 minutes.

3. Place a swordfish steak over each onion slice.

4. Thinly slice the lemon; discard the seeds and place the slices over the fish. Cover and cook on high for 45 minutes or until the fish is opaque. Transfer the (well-drained) fish to individual serving plates or to a serving platter.

5. In a small bowl, add the oil, lemon juice, mustard, and white or black pepper, if using, and whisk to combine.

6. Immediately before serving the swordfish, fold in the parsley. Evenly divide the sauce between the swordfish steaks.

PER SERVING: Calories: 274 | Fat: 14g | Protein: 34g | Sodium: 160mg | Fiber: 1g | Carbohydrates: 3g | Sugar: 1g

Manhattan Scallop Chowder

Serve this chowder with a tossed salad. Unlike the popular
New England version, this clam chowder is red!

INGREDIENTS | SERVES 6

2 tablespoons coconut butter, melted

2 stalks celery, finely diced

1 medium green bell pepper, seeded and diced

1 large carrot, peeled and finely diced

1 medium onion, peeled and diced

2 medium butternut squash or turnips, diced

1 (15-ounce) can diced tomatoes

1 (15-ounce) can tomato purée

2 cups bottled clam juice

1 cup dry white wine

¾ cup water

1 teaspoon dried thyme

1 teaspoon dried parsley

1 bay leaf

¼ teaspoon freshly ground black pepper

1½ pounds bay scallops

Fresh parsley, minced (optional)

Fresh basil (optional)

1. Add the butter, celery, bell pepper, and carrot to a 4- or 6-quart slow cooker; stir to coat the vegetables in the butter. Cover and cook on high for 15 minutes. Stir in the onion. Cover and cook on high for 30 minutes, or until the vegetables are soft.

2. Stir in the squash, tomatoes, tomato purée, clam juice, wine, water, thyme, parsley, bay leaf, and pepper. Cover, reduce the temperature to low, and cook for 7 hours or until the squash are cooked through.

3. Cut the scallops so that they are each no larger than 1-inch pieces. Add to the slow cooker.

4. Increase the temperature to high, cover, and cook for 15 minutes or until the scallops are firm.

5. Remove and discard the bay leaf. Taste for seasoning and adjust seasonings if necessary. Ladle into soup bowls. If desired, sprinkle minced parsley over each serving and garnish with basil.

PER SERVING: Calories: 188 | Fat: 1g | Protein: 21g | Sodium: 583mg | Fiber: 3g | Carbohydrates: 17g | Sugar: 7g

Hatteras Clam Chowder

This cozy, creamy Paleo chowder is thickened by turnips, in place of potatoes.
Serve it with a fresh green salad or hearty main dish of your choice.

INGREDIENTS | SERVES 4

1 small onion, diced and sautéed in olive oil (1 tablespoon)

2 medium turnips, peeled and diced

1 (8-ounce) bottle clam stock

2–3 cups water

½ teaspoon freshly ground black pepper

2 (6½-ounce) cans minced clams, undrained

1. Add cooked onions to a greased 2½-quart slow cooker.

2. Add turnips, clam stock, and enough water to cover (2–3 cups). Add pepper.

3. Cover and cook on high for 3 hours, until turnips are very tender.

4. One hour prior to serving, add in the clams along with broth from the cans and cook until heated through.

PER SERVING: Calories: 159 | Fat: 2g | Protein: 24g | Sodium: 149mg | Fiber: 1g | Carbohydrates: 10g | Sugar: 3g

Chapter 9

For the Vegetarian Paleo

Summer-Style Vegetarian Chili

*This light, meat-free chili is full of an array of summer vegetables. A very low-calorie,
high-fiber recipe loaded with vitamins and minerals.*

INGREDIENTS | SERVES 8

1 bulb fennel, diced

4 radishes, diced

2 stalks celery, diced, including leaves

2 large carrots, cut into coin-sized pieces

1 medium onion, diced

1 shallot, diced

4 cloves garlic, sliced

1 habanero pepper, diced

12 ounces tomato paste

½ teaspoon dried oregano

½ teaspoon freshly ground black pepper

½ teaspoon crushed rosemary

½ teaspoon cayenne pepper

½ teaspoon ground chipotle

1 teaspoon chili powder

1 teaspoon tarragon

¼ teaspoon cumin

¼ teaspoon celery seeds

2 zucchini, cubed

2 summer squash, cubed

10 Campari tomatoes, quartered

1. In a 4-quart slow cooker, add the fennel, radishes, celery, carrots, onion, shallot, garlic, habanero, tomato paste, and all the herbs and spices. Stir.

2. Cook on low for 6–7 hours; then stir in the zucchini, summer squash, and tomatoes. Cook on high for an additional 30 minutes. Stir before serving.

PER SERVING: Calories: 109 | Fat: 1g | Protein: 5g | Sodium: 386mg | Fiber: 7g | Carbohydrates: 24g | Sugar: 13g

Spiced "Baked" Eggplant

Serve this as a main dish over a garden salad, or as a side dish as is.

INGREDIENTS | SERVES 4

1 pound cubed eggplant

⅓ cup sliced onion

½ teaspoon red pepper flakes

½ teaspoon crushed rosemary

¼ cup lemon juice

Cold Snap

Take care not to put a cold ceramic slow cooker insert directly into the slow cooker. The sudden shift in temperature can cause it to crack. If you want to prepare your ingredients the night before use, refrigerate them in reusable containers, not in the insert.

Place all the ingredients in a 1½- to 2-quart slow cooker. Cook on low for 3 hours or until the eggplant is tender.

PER SERVING: Calories: 37 | Fat: 0g | Protein: 1g | Sodium: 6mg | Fiber: 4g | Carbohydrates: 9g | Sugar: 4g

Ratatouille

Ratatouille made in the slow cooker comes out surprisingly crisp-tender.

INGREDIENTS | SERVES 4

1 large onion, roughly chopped

1 eggplant, peeled and sliced horizontally

2 zucchini, sliced

1 cubanelle pepper, sliced

3 tomatoes, cut into wedges

2 tablespoons minced fresh basil

2 tablespoons minced fresh Italian parsley

½ teaspoon freshly ground black pepper

3 ounces tomato paste

¼ cup water

1. Place the onion, eggplant, zucchini, cubanelle pepper, and tomatoes into a 4-quart slow cooker. Sprinkle with basil, parsley, and black pepper.

2. In a small bowl, whisk the tomato paste and water together. Pour the mixture over the vegetables in the slow cooker. Stir.

3. Cook on low for 4 hours or until the eggplant and zucchini are fork-tender.

PER SERVING: Calories: 102 | Fat: 1g | Protein: 5g | Sodium: 185mg | Fiber: 9g | Carbohydrates: 23g | Sugar: 13g

Slow-Cooked Broccoli

A great way to cook a large amount of broccoli, while preserving all its nutrients.

INGREDIENTS | SERVES 5

1 pound fresh broccoli
½ cup water or chicken broth
2 tablespoons canola oil
½ teaspoon lemon juice
¼ teaspoon freshly ground black pepper

1. Cut the main stalk off of fresh broccoli with a sharp kitchen knife, and then rinse the broccoli under cool running water. Place the broccoli into a 2-quart slow cooker.

2. Pour water into the slow cooker with the broccoli. Add canola oil.

3. Add lemon juice and black pepper. Cover and cook on low for 3 hours or until the broccoli is tender.

4. Serve immediately or allow to stay warm in the cooker for another hour.

PER SERVING: Calories: 89 | Fat: 6g | Protein: 3g |
Sodium: 135mg | Fiber: 2g | Carbohydrates: 7g | Sugar: 2g

"Roasted" Roots

A perfect substitute for meats that typically call for a starchy side.

INGREDIENTS | SERVES 6

1 pound baby carrots

12 ounces turnips, peeled and cubed

1 medium onion, chopped

2 cloves garlic, minced

2 tablespoons water

3 tablespoons olive oil

¼ teaspoon lemon juice

⅛ teaspoon freshly ground black pepper

1. Combine the vegetables, water, olive oil, lemon juice, and pepper in a 3- to 4-quart slow cooker and stir to combine.

2. Cover and cook on low for 7–9 hours or until vegetables are tender when pierced with a fork.

PER SERVING: Calories: 110 | Fat: 7g | Protein: 1g | Sodium: 97mg | Fiber: 4g | Carbohydrates: 12g | Sugar: 6g

Caveman Caponata

An extremely flavorful, high-fiber, nutrient-dense vegetable entrée.
The high fiber content makes this meat-free dish very filling.

INGREDIENTS | SERVES 4

1 pound plum tomatoes, chopped

1 eggplant, cut into ½-inch pieces

2 medium zucchini, cut into ½-inch pieces

3 stalks celery, sliced

1 large onion, finely chopped

½ cup chopped parsley

1 teaspoon lemon juice

2 tablespoons lime juice

1 tablespoon honey

¼ cup raisins

¼ cup tomato paste

¼ teaspoon freshly ground black pepper

1. Combine tomatoes, eggplant, zucchini, celery, onion, parsley, lemon and lime juice, honey, raisins, tomato paste, and pepper in 4-quart slow cooker.

2. Cover and cook on low for 5½ hours. Do not remove cover during cooking.

PER SERVING: Calories: 129 | Fat: 1g | Protein: 4g | Sodium: 169mg | Fiber: 8g | Carbohydrates: 31g | Sugar: 20g

Zucchini Casserole

This highly nutritious and delicious vegetable compilation is the perfect lunch-time portion.

INGREDIENTS | SERVES 2

4 medium zucchini, unpeeled and sliced

1 red onion, sliced

1 green pepper, cut into thin strips

1 (15-ounce) can diced tomatoes, undrained

1 teaspoon lemon juice

½ teaspoon freshly ground black pepper

½ teaspoon basil

1 tablespoon canola oil

1. Combine all the ingredients except the canola oil in a 2-quart slow cooker. Cook on low for 3 hours.

2. Drizzle casserole with canola oil. Cook on low for 1½ hours more.

PER SERVING: Calories: 201 | Fat: 9g | Protein: 8g | Sodium: 356mg | Fiber: 8g | Carbohydrates: 30g | Sugar: 19g

Gone Nuts over Broccoli

A traditional "go-to" vegetable with a little kick! This recipe promises to prevent you from becoming bored with broccoli.

INGREDIENTS | SERVES 8

2 pounds broccoli florets, trimmed

12 cloves garlic, peeled

½ teaspoon freshly ground black pepper

1 cup large raw hazelnuts

2 tablespoons olive oil

Juice of 2 lemons

1. Place broccoli in a 4-quart slow cooker and add garlic, pepper, hazelnuts, olive oil, and lemon juice and toss.

2. Cover and cook on high for 2 hours or on low for 4 hours.

PER SERVING: Calories: 169 | Fat: 13g | Protein: 6g | Sodium: 38mg | Fiber: 5g | Carbohydrates: 13g | Sugar: 3g

Slow-Cooked Paleo-Stuffed Portobello

Portobello mushrooms are a rich source of antioxidants, all of which are generally preserved through cooking, unlike other vegetables whose phytonutrient compounds are often destroyed during the cooking process.

INGREDIENTS | SERVES 2

4 large portobello mushrooms, stems removed and chopped, centers removed

1½ cups cherry tomatoes, chopped

¼ cup arrowroot powder

3 tablespoons olive oil

¼ cup lime juice

1 tablespoon dried basil

½ teaspoon lemon juice

½ teaspoon freshly ground black pepper

1. Place mushroom centers and stems, tomatoes, arrowroot powder, olive oil, lime juice, basil, lemon juice, and pepper in a large mixing bowl. Mix well.

2. Place mushroom caps on bottom of a greased 6-quart oval slow cooker. Spoon mixture on top of mushrooms. Cover and cook on low for 4–7 hours.

PER SERVING: Calories: 261 | Fat: 21g | Protein: 1g | Sodium: 7mg | Fiber: 2g | Carbohydrates: 20g | Sugar: 3g

Sweet and Savory Acorn Squash

This rich-tasting, sweet side serves well as a substitute for the starch often called for in recipes.
This is so flavorful and filling, it can also suffice as a main lunch-time dish.

INGREDIENTS | SERVES 4

¾ cup honey

1 teaspoon ground cinnamon

1 teaspoon ground nutmeg

2 small acorn squash, halved and seeded

¾ cup raisins

4 tablespoons coconut butter

½ cup water

1. In a small bowl, combine the honey, cinnamon, and nutmeg.

2. Spoon honey mixture into the squash halves. Sprinkle with raisins.

3. Top each half with 1 tablespoon of the coconut butter.

4. Wrap each squash half individually in aluminum foil, and seal tightly.

5. Pour the water into a 4- to 6-quart slow cooker. Place the squash, cut-side up, in the slow cooker. Cover and cook on high for 4 hours or until the squash is tender.

6. Open the foil packets carefully to allow steam to escape.

PER SERVING: Calories: 280 | Fat: 0g | Protein: 1g | Sodium: 7mg | Fiber: 2g | Carbohydrates: 75g | Sugar: 68g

Acorn Squash Casserole

Try this recipe using other seasonal fall vegetables like butternut squash or eggplant.
Round out this classic comfort cuisine and serve with pumpkin or sweet potato soup.

INGREDIENTS | SERVES 6

2 medium acorn squash, peeled and sliced
1 red onion, sliced
1 green pepper, cut into strips
1 pound diced fresh tomatoes, unpeeled
1 teaspoon lemon juice
½ teaspoon freshly ground black pepper
½ teaspoon basil
1 tablespoon coconut oil

1. Combine all the ingredients except coconut oil in a 2-quart slow cooker.

2. Cover and cook on low for 3 hours.

3. Drizzle the casserole with coconut oil and cook another 1½ hours on low.

PER SERVING: Calories: 25 | Fat: 0g | Protein: 1g | Sodium: 5mg | Fiber: 2g | Carbohydrates: 6g | Sugar: 3g

Sautéed Fennel with Orange

Fennel is crunchy and a bit sweet, and is most often associated with Italian cuisine.

INGREDIENTS | SERVES 4

3 small fennel bulbs, halved
1 (13-ounce) can chopped tomatoes
Juice and zest of 1 small orange
2 tablespoons honey
Freshly ground black pepper, to taste

1. Place the halved fennel in a 4- to 6-quart slow cooker.

2. In a large mixing bowl, combine the remaining ingredients. Pour mixture over the fennel in the slow cooker.

3. Cover and cook on high for 4–5 hours.

PER SERVING: Calories: 59 | Fat: 0g | Protein: 1g | Sodium: 131mg | Fiber: 2g | Carbohydrates: 15g | Sugar: 13g

Vegetable Fajita Filling

Use large lettuce or cabbage leaves as the fajita "wrap,"
or serve over a starchy or seasonal root vegetable.

INGREDIENTS | SERVES 3

3 large onions, thinly sliced and separated

2 large sweet peppers (1 red and 1 green), julienned

2 tablespoons olive oil

½ teaspoon paprika

Freshly ground black pepper, to taste

1. Place all the ingredients into a 4- to 6-quart slow cooker and toss well.

2. Cover and cook on high for 3½–4 hours.

PER SERVING: (1 cup) | Calories: 163 | Fat: 9g | Protein: 3g | Sodium: 10mg | Fiber: 5g | Carbohydrates: 19g | Sugar: 9g

Spaghetti Squash and Garden Veggies

Spaghetti squash is frequently used as a pasta substitute in Paleo recipes, due to its similarities in appearance, texture, and taste.

INGREDIENTS | SERVES 2

1 spaghetti squash
1–2 cups water
2 tablespoons olive oil
1 large onion, diced
2 cloves garlic, minced
5 Roma or plum tomatoes, chopped
3 tablespoons chopped fresh basil
Freshly ground black pepper, to taste

1. Pierce the spaghetti squash several times with a fork. Place it in a 4- to 6-quart slow cooker and cover with 1–2 cups of water.

2. Cover and cook on low for 6–8 hours or on high for 3–4 hours. Remove from slow cooker and let it cool. Drain the water from the slow cooker.

3. While the squash is cooling, heat oil in a large nonstick skillet over medium-high heat. Sauté the onion for 5–10 minutes, until tender, and add the garlic and stir. Turn off heat.

4. Slice the cooked squash in half, seed it, and use a fork to shred the strands. Return the strands to the slow cooker.

5. Add the onion mixture to the slow cooker.

6. Add the tomatoes and toss so that they become warm.

7. Add the basil and toss. Serve warm and sprinkle with pepper to taste.

PER SERVING: Calories: 175 | Fat: 14g | Protein: 2g | Sodium: 18mg | Fiber: 3g | Carbohydrates: 12g | Sugar: 6g

Garlicky Vegetable Soup

Garlic is a versatile vegetable with multiple health benefits, such as its blood pressure and cholesterol-lowering capabilities, as well as its high antioxidant profile, which aids in reducing inflammation and lowering the risk of developing diseases like cancer.

INGREDIENTS | SERVES 4

5 heads garlic, peeled

6 cups Roasted Vegetable Stock (page 79)

1 (6-ounce) can tomato paste

1 large yellow onion, diced

¼ teaspoon lemon juice

2 tablespoons olive oil

Fresh basil, for garnish

1. Place all the ingredients except the oil and basil into a 4- to 6-quart slow cooker. Stir.

2. Cover and cook on low for 8 hours or on high for 5 hours.

3. Add olive oil. Use an immersion blender or blend the soup in batches in a standard blender until smooth.

4. Garnish with basil and serve.

PER SERVING: Calories: 120 | Fat: 7g | Protein: 2g | Sodium: 343mg | Fiber: 3g | Carbohydrates: 17g | Sugar: 8g

Baked Sweet Potatoes

The simplest way to prepare this carbohydrate-rich side dish, perfect for the Paleo athlete.

INGREDIENTS | SERVES 2

2 large sweet potatoes

1. Wash off the sweet potatoes but don't dry them. You'll want the moisture in the slow cooker.

2. Stab each sweet potato with a fork 5 or 6 times. Place the sweet potatoes in the slow cooker.

3. Cover and cook on low for 5–6 hours.

PER SERVING: Calories: 112 | Fat: 0g | Protein: 2g | Sodium: 72mg | Fiber: 4g | Carbohydrates: 26g | Sugar: 5g

Paleo "Pasta" Palooza

Serve this "pasta" tossed with fresh herbs, pepper, and your favorite Paleo-friendly sauce (see Chapter 4).

INGREDIENTS | SERVES 1

2 cups water
1 spaghetti squash

1. With a skewer or large fork, puncture several holes in the spaghetti squash.

2. Pour water into a 2-quart slow cooker and add the whole squash. Cover and cook on low for 8–9 hours.

3. Split the squash and remove the seeds. Use a fork to shred the strands from the squash, which will resemble angel hair pasta. Transfer the "spaghetti" strands to a bowl and top with sauce of your choice.

PER SERVING: Calories: 52 | Fat: 1g | Protein: 4g | Sodium: 6mg | Fiber: 4g | Carbohydrates: 11g | Sugar: 7g

Walnut-Stuffed Slow-Cooked Apples

Walnuts are an excellent source of omega-3s, vitamin E, and a variety of other phytonutrients and antioxidants.

INGREDIENTS | SERVES 4

¼ cup coarsely chopped walnuts
3 tablespoons dried currants
¾ teaspoon ground cinnamon, divided
4 medium Granny Smith apples, cored
1 cup honey
¾ cup apple cider

1. In a small bowl, combine first two ingredients. Add ¼ teaspoon cinnamon, stirring to combine.

2. Peel top third of each apple; place apples in a 2-quart or smaller slow cooker. Spoon walnut mixture into the cavity of each apple.

3. In a mixing bowl, combine the remaining ½ teaspoon cinnamon, honey, and apple cider, stirring to combine. Pour over apples in the slow cooker.

4. Cover and cook on low for 2¾ hours. Remove the apples with a slotted spoon.

5. Spoon ¼ cup cooking liquid over each serving.

PER SERVING: Calories: 264 | Fat: 0g | Protein: 0g | Sodium: 20mg | Fiber: 0g | Carbohydrates: 68g | Sugar: 66g

Apple and Sweet Potato Casserole

*This sweet and simple dish is loaded with vitamins C and A, and
would be perfect for Thanksgiving or even as a dessert!*

INGREDIENTS | SERVES 6

Nonstick cooking spray

4 large sweet potatoes, peeled and sliced

1 (15-ounce) can apple pie filling or Crustless Apple Pie (page 263)

2 tablespoons coconut butter, melted

Canned Shortcuts

Using apple pie filling in this recipe is an easy way to add apples, spices, and sweetness without a lot of hassle. Apple pie filling is good not only with sweet potatoes, but also with a breakfast dish or a Paleo-approved, slow-cooked cake or bread recipe.

1. Grease a 4-quart slow cooker with nonstick cooking spray. Place the sweet potatoes in the bottom of the slow cooker.

2. Add the apple pie filling and coconut butter to the slow cooker. Cover and cook on high for 3–4 hours, until the sweet potatoes are fork-tender.

PER SERVING: Calories: 75 | Fat: 0g | Protein: 1g | Sodium: 48mg | Fiber: 3g | Carbohydrates: 17g | Sugar: 4g

Herb-Stuffed Tomatoes

Serve these Italian-influenced stuffed tomatoes with a simple salad for an easy, light meal.

INGREDIENTS | SERVES 2

2 large tomatoes

1 stalk celery, minced

1 tablespoon minced fresh garlic

2 tablespoons minced fresh oregano

2 tablespoons minced fresh Italian parsley

1 teaspoon dried chervil

1 teaspoon fennel seeds

¾ cup water

1. Cut out the core of each tomato and discard. Scoop out the seeds, leaving the walls of the tomato intact.

2. In a small bowl, stir together the celery, garlic, and spices. Divide into two even portions, and stuff one portion into the center of each tomato.

3. Place the filled tomatoes in a single layer in a 4-quart slow cooker. Pour the water into the bottom of the slow cooker. Cook on low for 4 hours.

PER SERVING: Calories: 48 | Fat: 0g | Protein: 2g | Sodium: 29mg | Fiber: 3g | Carbohydrates: 10g | Sugar: 5g

Leek, Turnip, and Carrot Potage

Potage is a classic French home-style soup that is perfect for a blustery winter day.

INGREDIENTS | SERVES 6

4 cups sliced leeks

4 medium-sized (size of a potato) turnips, peeled and cubed

2 large carrots, peeled and diced

5 cups water

½ teaspoon white pepper

1. Place all the ingredients into a 4-quart slow cooker. Cook on low for 7 hours.

2. Purée using an immersion blender, or purée in batches in a standard blender. Serve piping hot.

PER SERVING: Calories: 69 | Fat: 0g | Protein: 2g | Sodium: 89mg | Fiber: 3g | Carbohydrates: 16g | Sugar: 6g

Chapter 10

Sides

"Steamed" Artichokes

Choose artichokes that are all the same size so they will finish cooking at the same time.

INGREDIENTS | SERVES 4

4 large artichokes

1 cup water

1 lemon, cut into eighths, seeds removed

2 tablespoons lemon juice

1 teaspoon dried oregano

1. Place the artichokes stem-side down in an oval 4-quart slow cooker. Pour the water into the bottom of the slow cooker. Add the lemon, lemon juice, and oregano.

2. Cook on low for 6 hours or until the leaves are tender.

PER SERVING: Calories: 83 | Fat: 0g | Protein: 6g | Sodium: 156mg | Fiber: 9g | Carbohydrates: 19g | Sugar: 2g

Poached Figs

Use these poached figs in any recipe that calls for cooked figs, or eat them as is.

INGREDIENTS | SERVES 4

8 ounces fresh figs

1 cup water

1 vanilla bean, split

1 tablespoon raw honey

1. Put all ingredients into a 2-quart slow cooker. Cook on low for 5 hours or until the figs are cooked through and starting to split.

2. Remove the figs from the poaching liquid and serve.

PER SERVING: Calories: 58 | Fat: 0g | Protein: 0g | Sodium: 3mg | Fiber: 2g | Carbohydrates: 15g | Sugar: 13g

Shopping for Figs

Look for figs that are plump and soft but not squishy. The skin should not be split or oozing. Store figs in the refrigerator or in a cool dark cabinet until ready to use.

Roasted Garlic

*Roasted garlic is mellow enough to eat as is, but it is also great
in any recipe that would benefit from a mild garlic flavor.*

INGREDIENTS | YIELDS 4 HEADS OF GARLIC

½ tablespoon olive oil

4 heads garlic

1. Pour the oil into the bottom of a 2-quart slow cooker. Place the garlic in a single layer on top of the oil.

2. Cook on low for 4–6 hours or until the garlic is very soft and golden. To serve, simply squeeze the garlic out of the skin.

PER SERVING: (1 tablespoon) | Calories: 15 | Fat: 2g | Protein: 0g | Sodium: 0mg | Fiber: 0g | Carbohydrates: 0g | Sugar: 0g

Caramelized Onions

*So sweet it feels like dessert! Serve over beef or pork as
a sweet way to complement a basic traditional dish.*

INGREDIENTS | SERVES 2

Nonstick cooking spray

1 extra large onion, peeled and thinly sliced

1 tablespoon olive oil

1 clove garlic, minced

1. Spray the insert of a 3- to 4-quart slow cooker with nonstick spray, add ingredients in order listed, stir, and cover.

2. Cook on high for 10–12 hours.

PER SERVING: Calories: 62 | Fat: 7g | Protein: 0g | Sodium: 0mg | Fiber: 0g | Carbohydrates: 1g | Sugar: 0g

Blackberry Compote

Try this on slow-cooked pineapple or apples.

INGREDIENTS | SERVES 6

2 cups blackberries

¼ cup raw honey

¼ cup water

Place all ingredients into a 2-quart slow cooker. Cover and cook on low for 3 hours, remove the lid, and cook on high for 4 hours.

PER SERVING: Calories: 64 | Fat: 0g | Protein: 1g | Sodium: 1mg | Fiber: 3g | Carbohydrates: 16g | Sugar: 14g

Strawberry-Rhubarb Compote

Try this over fruit salad or another sweet treat.

INGREDIENTS | YIELDS 1½ CUPS

1 pound strawberries, diced

½ pound rhubarb, diced

2 tablespoons lemon juice

1 tablespoon lemon zest

Rhubarb Facts

The leaves of the rhubarb plant are toxic, but the stalks are perfectly edible. Despite being a tart vegetable, rhubarb is most often served in sweet dishes where its tartness contrasts with a sweeter ingredient like strawberries.

1. Place all ingredients into a 3½- to 4-quart slow cooker. Cook on low for 2 hours.

2. Lightly mash with a potato masher.

3. Cook on high, uncovered, for 1 additional hour.

PER SERVING: Calories: 201 | Fat: 2g | Protein: 5g | Sodium: 20mg | Fiber: 13g | Carbohydrates: 48g | Sugar: 25g

Dill Carrots

The carrots in this side dish keep a firm texture even when fully cooked.

INGREDIENTS | SERVES 6

1 pound carrots, cut into coin-sized pieces
1 tablespoon minced fresh dill
⅓ teaspoon olive or canola oil
3 tablespoons water

Dill Details

Dill is a delicate plant that has many culinary uses. The seeds are used as a spice, and fresh and dried dill, called dill weed, are used as herbs. Dill is an essential ingredient in dill pickles and gravlax, a type of cured salmon.

1. Place all the ingredients into a 2-quart slow cooker. Stir. Cook on low 1½–2 hours or until the carrots are fork-tender.

2. Stir before serving.

PER SERVING: Calories: 31 | Fat: 0g | Protein: 1g | Sodium: 53mg | Fiber: 2g | Carbohydrates: 7g | Sugar: 4g

Slow-Cooked Brussels Sprouts

A traditional "not-so-favorite" turned decadent and delicious!

INGREDIENTS | SERVES 4

1 pound Brussels sprouts, trimmed
¾ cup Chicken Stock (page 78)
2 tablespoons canola oil
3 tablespoons coconut butter
3 tablespoons finely chopped shallots

1. Place Brussels sprouts into a 4- to 6-quart slow cooker and pour the chicken stock over them.

2. Add the canola oil, coconut butter, and shallots.

3. Cover and cook on low for 3 hours or until sprouts are tender.

PER SERVING: Calories: 120 | Fat: 7g | Protein: 4g | Sodium: 33mg | Fiber: 4g | Carbohydrates: 12g | Sugar: 3g

Rosemary-Thyme Green Beans

In this recipe, the slow cooker acts like a steamer, resulting in tender, crisp green beans.

INGREDIENTS | SERVES 4

1 pound green beans
1 tablespoon minced rosemary
1 teaspoon minced thyme
2 tablespoons lemon juice
2 tablespoons water

1. Place all the ingredients into a 2-quart slow cooker. Stir to distribute the herbs evenly.

2. Cook on low for 1½ hours or until the green beans are tender. Stir before serving.

PER SERVING: Calories: 40 | Fat: 0g | Protein: 2g | Sodium: 9mg | Fiber: 4g | Carbohydrates: 9g | Sugar: 4g

Stewed Tomatoes

For an Italian variation on these tomatoes, add basil and Italian parsley.

INGREDIENTS | SERVES 6

1 (28-ounce) can whole tomatoes in purée, cut up
1 tablespoon minced onion
1 stalk celery, diced
½ teaspoon oregano
½ teaspoon thyme

Place all the ingredients into a 2-quart slow cooker. Stir. Cook on low for up to 8 hours.

PER SERVING: Calories: 24 | Fat: 0g | Protein: 1g | Sodium: 192mg | Fiber: 2g | Carbohydrates: 6g | Sugar: 3g

Stewed Cinnamon Apples

These apples are wonderful with pork. The longer they are cooked, the softer they become.

INGREDIENTS | SERVES 4

1 teaspoon honey
1 tablespoon ground cinnamon
2 tablespoons lemon juice
2 tablespoons water
4 crisp apples, cut into wedges

1. Place the honey, cinnamon, lemon juice, and water into a 4-quart slow cooker. Stir until the honey dissolves. Add the apples.

2. Cook on low for up to 8 hours. Stir before serving.

PER SERVING: Calories: 88 | Fat: 0g | Protein: 1g | Sodium: 2mg | Fiber: 3g | Carbohydrates: 24g | Sugar: 18g

Fig and Ginger Spread

Use as a breakfast fruit spread atop a Paleo breakfast bread recipe, or to liven up a basic Paleo dessert.

INGREDIENTS | SERVES 25

2 pounds fresh figs
2 tablespoons minced fresh ginger
2 tablespoons lime juice
½ cup water
¾ cup honey

1. Place all the ingredients in a 2-quart slow cooker. Stir. Cover and cook on low for 2–3 hours. Remove the lid and cook an additional 2–3 hours, until the mixture is thickened.

2. Pour into airtight containers and refrigerate for up to 6 weeks.

PER SERVING: Calories: 58 | Fat: 0g | Protein: 0g | Sodium: 1mg | Fiber: 1g | Carbohydrates: 15g | Sugar: 14g

Apple and Pear Spread

Make the most of in-season apples and pears in this easy alternative to apple or pear butter.

INGREDIENTS | YIELDS 3 QUARTS

4 Winesap apples, peeled, cored, and sliced

4 Bartlett pears, peeled, cored, and sliced

1 cup water or pear cider

½ cup honey

¼ teaspoon ginger

¼ teaspoon cinnamon

¼ teaspoon nutmeg

¼ teaspoon allspice

1. Place all the ingredients into a 4-quart slow cooker. Cover and cook on low for 10–12 hours.

2. Uncover and cook on low for an additional 10–12 hours or until thick and most of the liquid has evaporated.

3. Allow to cool completely, then pour into the food processor and purée. Pour into clean glass jars. Refrigerate for up to 6 weeks.

PER SERVING: (½ cup) | Calories: 35 | Fat: 0g | Protein: 0g | Sodium: 1mg | Fiber: 0g | Carbohydrates: 9g | Sugar: 9g

Honey-Drizzled Brussels Sprouts and Pearl Onions

*A sweeter, more fun way to enjoy vegetables. You'll be surprised how quickly
your family asks for "more Brussels sprouts!"*

INGREDIENTS | SERVES 4

8 ounces small Brussels sprouts

8 ounces frozen pearl onions, thawed

1¼ cups water

1 tablespoon canola or flaxseed oil

¼ cup honey

White pepper, to taste

1. In a 4-quart slow cooker, add Brussels sprouts, onions, and water. Cover and cook on high for about 2 hours or until Brussels sprouts are soft. Drain.

2. Add the oil and honey to the cooked sprouts. Cover and cook on high for about 10 minutes, or until glazed.

3. Season to taste with white pepper.

PER SERVING: Calories: 89 | Fat: 0g | Protein: 2g | Sodium: 17mg | Fiber: 2g | Carbohydrates: 23g | Sugar: 19g

Greek-Style Asparagus

A slight Mediterranean touch induces a delicious aroma.

INGREDIENTS | SERVES 8

1 pound asparagus, trimmed

1 (28-ounce) can petite-diced tomatoes, undrained

½ cup chopped onion

4 cloves garlic, minced

¾ teaspoon dried oregano

¾ teaspoon basil

Freshly ground black pepper, to taste

1. Combine all the ingredients except pepper in a 2-quart or smaller slow cooker and cover.

2. Cook on high for about 4½ hours or until the asparagus is tender. Season to taste with pepper.

PER SERVING: Calories: 17 | Fat: 0g | Protein: 1g | Sodium: 2mg | Fiber: 1g | Carbohydrates: 4g | Sugar: 2g

Sweet Beets

New research has shown an association between nitrates, such as those naturally occurring in beets, and increased performance in endurance sports. Serve this dish warm alongside roast pork or beef, or cold with sliced meats.

INGREDIENTS | SERVES 6

1½ pounds beets

2 cups hot water

¼ cup finely chopped red onion

¼ cup honey

2 cloves garlic, minced

¼ cup raisins

4 tablespoons toasted walnuts

2–3 tablespoons lemon juice

1 tablespoon coconut oil

Freshly ground black pepper, to taste

1. Combine the beets and water in a 4- to 6-quart slow cooker. Cover and cook on high for about 2–2½ hours or until the beets are tender.

2. Drain and peel the beets, and cut into ¾-inch cubes. Combine cubed beets and remaining ingredients except pepper in the slow cooker.

3. Cover and cook on high for 20–30 minutes. Season with pepper to taste.

PER SERVING: Calories: 147 | Fat: 3g | Protein: 3g | Sodium: 93mg | Fiber: 4g | Carbohydrates: 29g | Sugar: 23g

Tangy Green Beans

This versatile side dish can dress up just about any meal.
Try adding additional ingredients like slivered almonds or cranberries.

INGREDIENTS | SERVES 4

4 cups frozen green beans, thawed
¼ cup chopped onion
¼ cup chopped green bell pepper
¼ cup lime juice
2 tablespoons honey
⅛ teaspoon freshly ground black pepper

1. Combine all the ingredients in a 2-quart or smaller slow cooker. Stir to distribute evenly.

2. Cover and cook on low for 5 hours. Serve warm.

PER SERVING: Calories: 72 | Fat: 0g | Protein: 2g | Sodium: 8mg | Fiber: 3g | Carbohydrates: 18g | Sugar: 13g

Slow-Cooker Cabbage

This high-fiber, low-calorie vegetable is rich in antioxidants and an excellent source of vitamins C and K.

INGREDIENTS | SERVES 3

1 large head of red cabbage, coarsely sliced
6 tart apples, cored and quartered
2 medium onions, coarsely chopped
2 cups hot water
⅔ cup lime juice
6 tablespoons coconut butter
3 tablespoons honey
2 teaspoons lemon juice

1. Place all the ingredients in a 2-quart slow cooker.

2. Cover and cook on low for 8–10 hours or on high for 3 hours. Stir well before serving.

PER SERVING: Calories: 325 | Fat: 1g | Protein: 6g | Sodium: 64mg | Fiber: 13g | Carbohydrates: 83g | Sugar: 63g

Pumpkin Butter

Serve with apple slices, pear slices, drizzled over butternut squash
or on top of a Paleo-friendly dessert of your choice.

INGREDIENTS | SERVES 8

6 cups pumpkin purée
2¼ cups honey
1 teaspoon cinnamon
¾ teaspoon ground ginger
½ teaspoon ground cloves
¼ teaspoon ground nutmeg
Juice of 3 lemons

1. Add all the ingredients to a 4- to 6-quart slow cooker. Cook the mixture on low for about 4–4½ hours, until it becomes thick and smooth.

2. Pour the finished pumpkin butter into sterilized pint or half pint jars, and seal.

PER SERVING: Calories: 298 | Fat: 0g | Protein: 1g | Sodium: 5mg | Fiber: 1g | Carbohydrates: 81g | Sugar: 79g

Glazed Carrots

The slow cooker is an excellent way of preparing carrots,
just be sure to allow enough time for them to cook.

INGREDIENTS | SERVES 3

3 cups thinly sliced carrots
2 cups water
¼ teaspoon lemon juice
3 tablespoons coconut butter
2 tablespoons chopped pecans
3 tablespoons honey

1. Combine carrots, water, and lemon juice in 2-quart or smaller slow cooker. Cover and cook on high for 2–3 hours or until the carrots are fork tender.

2. Drain well; stir in the remaining ingredients.

3. Cover and cook on high for 20–30 minutes.

PER SERVING: Calories: 141 | Fat: 4g | Protein: 2g | Sodium: 82mg | Fiber: 4g | Carbohydrates: 29g | Sugar: 23g

Carrot Nutmeg Pudding

Carrots are often served as a savory side dish. In this recipe the carrots have just a little bit of honey added to bring out their natural sweetness.

INGREDIENTS | SERVES 4

4 large carrots, grated
2 tablespoons coconut butter
½ teaspoon freshly grated nutmeg
2 tablespoons honey
1 teaspoon vanilla
1 cup coconut milk
3 eggs, beaten

1. Add carrots and coconut butter to a large glass, microwavable bowl. Cook on high for 3–4 minutes, until carrots are slightly softened.

2. Stir in remaining ingredients and pour into a greased 2½-quart slow cooker. Cook on high for 3 hours or on low for 6 hours. Serve hot or cold.

PER SERVING: Calories: 231 | Fat: 16g | Protein: 6g | Sodium: 110mg | Fiber: 2g | Carbohydrates: 18g | Sugar: 13g

Butternut Squash with Walnuts and Vanilla

Butternut squash has a very mild and slightly sweet flavor. Often people who don't like sweet potatoes enjoy this alternative side dish. Many grocery stores now sell butternut squash that has been peeled and precut into cubes, which can make meal preparation a breeze.

INGREDIENTS | SERVES 4

Nonstick cooking spray
1 butternut squash (about 2 pounds), peeled, seeds removed, and cut into 1-inch cubes
½ cup water
½ cup honey
1 cup chopped walnuts
1 teaspoon cinnamon
4 tablespoons coconut butter
2 teaspoons grated ginger
1 teaspoon vanilla

1. Grease a 4-quart slow cooker with nonstick cooking spray. Add the cubed butternut squash and water to slow cooker.

2. In a small bowl, mix together the honey, walnuts, cinnamon, coconut butter, ginger, and vanilla. Drizzle this honey mixture evenly over the butternut squash.

3. Cook on high for 4 hours or on low for 6–8 hours, until the butternut squash is fork-tender.

PER SERVING: Calories: 328 | Fat: 19g | Protein: 5g | Sodium: 4mg | Fiber: 2g | Carbohydrates: 40g | Sugar: 36g

Sweet and Sour Red Cabbage

Cabbage is often overlooked when it comes to weekly meals, which is unfortunate considering how nutritious it is. The tart apples, honey, and lime juice give the cabbage a tangy pickled flavor. Try this recipe as a side to roast pork.

INGREDIENTS | SERVES 6

1 large head red cabbage, sliced

2 medium onions, chopped

6 small tart apples, peeled (if preferred), cored, and quartered

1 cup hot water

1 cup apple juice

⅓ cup honey

⅔ cup lime juice

½ teaspoon caraway seeds

3 tablespoons coconut butter, melted

3 tablespoons canola oil

1. Place the cabbage, onions, and apples into a greased 4-quart slow cooker.

2. In a medium bowl, whisk together the water, apple juice, honey, lime juice, and caraway seeds. Pour over the cabbage.

3. Drizzle coconut butter and canola oil over everything and cover slow cooker. Cook on high for 3–4 hours or on low for 6–8 hours. Stir well before serving.

PER SERVING: Calories: 253 | Fat: 7g | Protein: 3g | Sodium: 32mg | Fiber: 6g | Carbohydrates: 49g | Sugar: 39g

Lemon-Garlic Green Beans

Lemon zest and sliced garlic add a fresh and bright flavor to these slow-cooked green beans. Fresh green beans are sturdy enough to withstand very long cooking times without getting mushy.

INGREDIENTS | SERVES 4

1½ pounds fresh green beans, trimmed

3 tablespoons olive oil

3 large shallots, cut into thin wedges

6 cloves garlic, sliced

1 tablespoon grated lemon zest

½ teaspoon freshly ground black pepper

½ cup water

1. Place the green beans in a greased 4-quart slow cooker. Add the remaining ingredients over the top of the beans.

2. Cook on high for 4–6 hours or on low for 8–10 hours. If you like your beans more crisp, check them on high after about 3½ hours or on low after about 6 hours.

PER SERVING: Calories: 150 | Fat: 11g | Protein: 3g | Sodium: 12mg | Fiber: 5g | Carbohydrates: 14g | Sugar: 6g

Honey-Ginger Carrots

Carrots and honey are a naturally delicious pair. Honey brings out the pure sweetness in baby carrots, and fresh ginger gives this dish extra bite!

INGREDIENTS | SERVES 4

1 (16-ounce) package baby carrots, peeled

2 tablespoons freshly squeezed orange juice

1 tablespoon honey

½ teaspoon freshly grated ginger

1 tablespoon orange zest

1 tablespoon fresh parsley

Storing Orange, Lemon, and Lime Zest

To keep fresh citrus zest on hand at all times, freeze it! Place zest in snack-sized zip-top bags and take out as much as you need when it's called for in a recipe. The zest should stay fresh for up to 6 months in the freezer.

1. Place the baby carrots in a greased 2½-quart slow cooker.

2. In a small bowl, mix together orange juice, honey, ginger, and orange zest. Pour over carrots. Cook on high for 3–4 hours or on low for 6–7 hours, until carrots are fork-tender.

3. Serve carrots by spooning a little bit of the honey-orange sauce over them and then sprinkling a little bit of fresh parsley over each plate.

PER SERVING: Calories: 58 | Fat: 0g | Protein: 1g | Sodium: 88mg | Fiber: 3g | Carbohydrates: 14g | Sugar: 10g

Stuffed Onions

Serve these onions with a salad and a steamed vegetable.

INGREDIENTS | SERVES 4

4 medium onions, peeled
1 pound ground beef or lamb
¼ teaspoon ground allspice
¼ teaspoon dried dill
3 tablespoons fresh lemon juice, divided
2 teaspoons dried parsley
Freshly ground black pepper, to taste
1 large egg
1–2 tablespoons almond flour
2 tablespoons extra-virgin olive oil
1 cup chicken broth

1. Cutting across the onions (not from bottom to top), cut the onions in half. Scoop out the onion cores.

2. Chop the onion cores and add to the ground beef or lamb, allspice, dill, 2 tablespoons of the lemon juice, parsley, pepper, and egg; mix well.

3. Fill the onion halves with the meat mixture. (The meat will overflow the onions and form a mound on top.) Sprinkle the almond flour over the top of the meat.

4. Add the oil to a deep 3½-quart nonstick skillet or electric skillet and bring it to temperature over medium heat. Add the onions to the pan, meat side down, and sauté for 10 minutes or until browned.

5. Arrange the onions in a 4-quart slow cooker so that the meat side is up. Mix the remaining tablespoon of lemon juice into the broth; pour the broth around the onions. Cover and cook on high for 4 hours, on low for 8 hours, or until the onion is soft and the meat is cooked through.

PER SERVING: Calories: 367 | Fat: 22g | Protein: 27g | Sodium: 361mg | Fiber: 2g | Carbohydrates: 15g | Sugar: 5g

Moroccan Root Vegetables

Moroccan Root Vegetables make an excellent side to a slow-cooked chicken or pork dish.

INGREDIENTS | SERVES 8

1 pound parsnips, peeled and diced
1 pound turnips, peeled and diced
2 medium onions, chopped
1 pound carrots, peeled and diced
6 dried apricots, chopped
4 pitted prunes, chopped
1 teaspoon ground turmeric
1 teaspoon ground cumin
½ teaspoon ground ginger
½ teaspoon ground cinnamon
¼ teaspoon cayenne pepper
1 tablespoon dried parsley
1 tablespoon dried cilantro
14 ounces vegetable broth

1. Add the parsnips, turnips, onions, carrots, apricots, prunes, turmeric, cumin, ginger, cinnamon, cayenne pepper, parsley, and cilantro to the slow cooker.

2. Pour in the vegetable broth. Cover and cook on low for 9 hours or until the vegetables are cooked through.

PER SERVING: Calories: 118 | Fat: 1g | Protein: 2g | Sodium: 85mg | Fiber: 7g | Carbohydrates: 28g | Sugar: 13g

"Mashed" Cauliflower

Use as a starch substitute in any recipe calling for potatoes, rice, pasta, or polenta to make it a Paleo-friendly meal.

INGREDIENTS | SERVES 4

1 head cauliflower, steamed and drained
1 tablespoon coconut butter
Freshly ground black pepper, to taste

Process cauliflower in a food processor with coconut butter and pepper until smooth. Serve warm.

PER SERVING: Calories: 36 | Fat: 0g | Protein: 3g | Sodium: 43mg | Fiber: 3g | Carbohydrates: 7g | Sugar: 3g

Chapter 11

For the Little Caveman: Kid-Friendly

Mini Caveman Squash (Baby Food)

This recipe makes about 6 servings (or fewer), depending on age and appetite!

INGREDIENTS | SERVES 3–6

2 yellow squash, peeled and cubed
¼ cup water

1. Place the squash in a 4- to 6-quart slow cooker, add water, cover, and cook on high for 3 hours.

2. Use a blender or food processor to purée into baby food.

PER SERVING: Calories: 21 | Fat: 0g | Protein: 2g | Sodium: 3mg | Fiber: 1g | Carbohydrates: 4g | Sugar: 3g

Mini Caveman Green Beans (Baby Food)

This recipe can be doubled, or even tripled, depending on how many "little cavemen" are at home, and how far ahead you wish to plan for.

INGREDIENTS | SERVES 6

1 (12-ounce) package frozen green beans
¼ cup water

1. Place the green beans in a 4- to 6-quart slow cooker, add water, cover, and cook on high for 3 hours.

2. Use a blender or food processor to purée into baby food.

PER SERVING: Calories: 17 | Fat: 0g | Protein: 1g | Sodium: 4mg | Fiber: 2g | Carbohydrates: 4g | Sugar: 2g

Mini Caveman Sweet Potatoes (Baby Food)

Turnips or winter squash could also be used here, in place of the sweet potatoes.

INGREDIENTS | SERVES 6

2 medium sweet potatoes

¾ cup water

1. Place the sweet potatoes in a 4- to 6-quart slow cooker, add water, cover, and cook on high for 3 hours.

2. Use a blender or food processor to purée into baby food.

PER SERVING: Calories: 37 | Fat: 0g | Protein: 1g | Sodium: 25mg | Fiber: 1g | Carbohydrates: 9g | Sugar: 2g

Mini Caveman Carrots (Baby Food)

This could also be used to incorporate puréed carrots into another recipe—to thicken a soup, for example.

INGREDIENTS | SERVES 6

12 ounces carrot sticks, thinly sliced and chopped

¼ cup water

1. Place the carrots in a 4- to 6-quart slow cooker, add water, cover, and cook on high for 3 hours.

2. Use a blender or food processor to purée into baby food.

PER SERVING: Calories: 23 | Fat: 0g | Protein: 1g | Sodium: 39mg | Fiber: 2g | Carbohydrates: 5g | Sugar: 3g

Stewed Fruit

An easy way to help the little ones at home meet their five-a-day fruit and vegetable needs.
This recipe is jam-packed with vitamin C and fiber.

INGREDIENTS | SERVES 6

1 pound prunes, pitted

8 ounces dried apricots

8 ounces dried pears

3 cups water

½ cup honey

2 tablespoons fresh lemon juice

1 teaspoon finely grated lemon zest

½ vanilla bean or ½ teaspoon vanilla extract

1. Combine all the ingredients together in a 2-quart slow cooker. Cook on low until the fruit is tender, 6–8 hours.

2. Serve warm or at room temperature.

PER SERVING: Calories: 379 | Fat: 1g | Protein: 3g | Sodium: 11mg | Fiber: 9g | Carbohydrates: 101g | Sugar: 75g

Chicken Tenders

A Paleo-approved version of a traditional kid-friendly favorite.
Partners perfectly with a side of Turnip Tots (page 206).

INGREDIENTS | SERVES 4

2 tablespoons olive oil

1 clove garlic, minced

6 sprigs fresh thyme, stripped and chopped

1 tablespoon lemon zest

¼ cup lemon juice

1 pound chicken breast tenders

Freshly ground black pepper, to taste

Nonstick cooking spray

1. In a large mixing bowl, combine the olive oil, garlic, chopped thyme, lemon zest, and lemon juice.

2. Season the chicken tenders with pepper.

3. Spray a 2-quart slow cooker with nonstick cooking spray. Place chicken in the slow cooker, and pour olive oil mixture over chicken, stirring until coated.

4. Cover and cook on low for 4–6 hours.

PER SERVING: Calories: 65 | Fat: 7g | Protein: 0g | Sodium: 4mg | Fiber: 0g | Carbohydrates: 2g | Sugar: 0g

"Roasted" Root Veggies

You won't have to beg the kids to eat their veggies with this yummy recipe.
You won't even have to ask them twice!

INGREDIENTS | SERVES 10

1½ pounds sweet potatoes
1 pound parsnips
1 pound carrots
2 large red onions, coarsely chopped
¾ cup sliced cranberries
1 tablespoon honey
3 tablespoons olive oil
2 tablespoons lemon juice
½ teaspoon freshly ground black pepper
⅓ cup chopped fresh flat-leaf parsley

1. Peel the sweet potatoes, parsnips, and carrots and cut into 1½-inch pieces.

2. Combine the parsnips, carrots, onions, and cranberries in a lightly greased 6-quart slow cooker; layer sweet potatoes over the top.

3. In a small bowl, mix together the honey, olive oil, lemon juice, and pepper; pour over vegetable mixture. (Do not stir.)

4. Cover and cook on high for 4–5 hours or until vegetables are tender. Toss with parsley just before serving.

PER SERVING: Calories: 193 | Fat: 4g | Protein: 2g | Sodium: 75mg | Fiber: 7g | Carbohydrates: 38g | Sugar: 16g

Turnip Tots

A Paleo-approved substitute for "Tater Tots," and the perfect accompaniment to Paleo Chicken Tenders (page 204). Serve with Homemade Ketchup (page 73).

INGREDIENTS | SERVES 4

4 medium turnips, peeled and cubed

2 tablespoons canola oil

2 tablespoons honey

1 tablespoon brown mustard

¼ teaspoon freshly ground black pepper

1. Place the turnips in a 2- or 4-quart slow cooker, drizzle with canola oil, and toss.

2. In a small bowl, mix together the remaining ingredients, drizzle over turnips, and toss.

3. Cover and cook on low for 5 hours. Serve alongside chicken tenders.

PER SERVING: Calories: 127 | Fat: 7g | Protein: 1g | Sodium: 82mg | Fiber: 2g | Carbohydrates: 17g | Sugar: 13g

Good Ol' Fashioned AB & J! (Almond Butter and Jelly)

Combine the finished product with some Strawberry Jelly (page 37), and there you have an AB & J!

INGREDIENTS | YIELDS 16 OUNCES

2 cups almonds

Olive oil, as needed (about 2–3 teaspoons)

1. Place almonds in food processor and turn on.

2. Add olive oil as needed, depending on creaminess desired.

3. Serve almond butter "sandwiches" by using frozen banana slices or apple slices, and smoothing almond butter and jelly between two fruit slices (or any other Paleo-friendly, creative version).

PER SERVING: (1 ounce of almond butter) | Calories: 68 | Fat: 6g | Protein: 3g | Sodium: 0mg | Fiber: 1g | Carbohydrates: 3g | Sugar: 0g

Paleo Stuffed Peppers

Peppers are chock-full of great vitamins and minerals that kids need.
These peppers are so fun to eat, kids won't know how healthy they are.

INGREDIENTS | SERVES 4

4 red bell peppers
2 tablespoons olive oil
3 cloves garlic, chopped
1 large onion, chopped
1 pound ground chicken
2 green bell peppers, chopped
1 cup diced celery
1 cup sliced mushrooms
2 tablespoons chili powder
1 tablespoon cumin
1 (28-ounce) can organic, no-salt-added diced tomatoes
1 (6-ounce) can organic, no-salt-added tomato paste

1. Cut off the tops of red peppers and remove seeds and ribs. Set aside.

2. In skillet, heat the olive oil and sauté garlic and onion for 2 minutes.

3. Add ground chicken and cook until browned, about 5 minutes.

4. Add green peppers, celery, mushrooms, chili powder, and cumin, and continue cooking for 5 minutes.

5. Stuff mixture into red peppers and place in a 4-quart slow cooker.

6. Pour diced tomatoes and tomato paste over peppers and cook on high for 5 hours.

PER SERVING: Calories: 385 | Fat: 25g | Protein: 23g | Sodium: 159mg | Fiber: 6g | Carbohydrates: 17g | Sugar: 9g

Soft "Shell" Beef Tacos

The romaine leaves could also be placed on the broiler until crispy, for use as a "hard" taco shell.

INGREDIENTS | SERVES 12

2 (16-ounce) jars mild or medium tomato-based salsa

2 tablespoons lime juice

5 teaspoons chili powder

1½ pounds beef chuck pot roast, fat trimmed

12 large leaves romaine lettuce (for use as taco "shells")

3 cups shredded lettuce

1 avocado, diced

1. Spoon 1 cup salsa into a small bowl; set aside.

2. In a 4-quart slow cooker, combine remaining salsa with lime juice and chili powder.

3. Add beef, cover, and cook on low for 10–12 hours. Shred the meat, using two forks, and spoon into a serving bowl.

4. Lay out the romaine leaves for use as taco "shells," and place a small portion of slow-cooked beef on each.

5. Place shredded lettuce, diced avocado, and reserved salsa in small separate bowls for serving. Add toppings to tacos, wrap lettuce leaves tight, and enjoy.

PER SERVING: Calories: 56 | Fat: 3g | Protein: 2g | Sodium: 464mg | Fiber: 3g | Carbohydrates: 8g | Sugar: 3g

Slow-Cooked Sloppy Joeys

Serve over mashed cauliflower, turnips, or winter squash.

INGREDIENTS | SERVES 4

1 pound lean ground beef or turkey

1 (6-ounce) can tomato paste

2 tablespoons honey

1 teaspoon lemon juice

1 tablespoon dried onion flakes

1 tablespoon paprika

1 teaspoon cumin

½ teaspoon garlic powder

¼ teaspoon dry mustard

¼ teaspoon celery seeds

¼ teaspoon freshly ground black pepper

1 cup warm water

1 teaspoon almond meal

1. Place meat, tomato paste, honey, lemon juice, and seasonings into a 4-quart slow cooker. Add water and almond meal, and stir.

2. Cover and cook on low for 6–7 hours or on high for 3–5 hours. Serve warm.

PER SERVING: Calories: 234 | Fat: 6g | Protein: 26g | Sodium: 414mg | Fiber: 3g | Carbohydrates: 18g | Sugar: 14g

Slow-Cooked Burgers

Serve these no-bun Paleo burgers with Sweet Potato "Fries"
(below) and Homemade Ketchup (page 73).

INGREDIENTS | SERVES 2

2 (4-ounce) pre-formed lean hamburger patties, frozen

⅛ teaspoon lemon juice

¼ teaspoon onion powder

¼ teaspoon dried basil

¼ teaspoon dried thyme

¼ teaspoon dried oregano

1. Insert a wire rack into a 6-quart slow cooker and place frozen patties on rack.

2. Drizzle lemon juice and seasonings on top.

3. Cover and cook on high for 60–90 minutes. Drain on paper towels before serving. Serve with slow-cooked Sweet Potato "Fries" (below).

PER SERVING: Calories: 318 | Fat: 26g | Protein: 19g | Sodium: 77mg | Fiber: 0g | Carbohydrates: 0g | Sugar: 0g

Sweet Potato "Fries"

Serve alongside a Slow-Cooked Burger (above) and drizzle with Homemade Ketchup
(page 73), honey, or some honey mustard.

INGREDIENTS | SERVES 2

2 medium sweet potatoes, sliced into thin wedges

¼ cup water

2 tablespoons canola oil

1. Place sweet potato wedges into a 4-quart slow cooker and add water.

2. Drizzle canola oil over sweet potatoes.

3. Cover and cook on high for 2–3 hours. Remove cover and continue cooking for 20–30 minutes, until desired browning occurs.

4. Serve alongside Slow-Cooked Burgers (above).

PER SERVING: Calories: 232 | Fat: 14g | Protein: 2g | Sodium: 72mg | Fiber: 4g | Carbohydrates: 26g | Sugar: 5g

Lemonade

Serve cold on a hot summer day, or warm on a cold winter's night!

INGREDIENTS | SERVES 6 (1-CUP SERVINGS)

5 cups water
¾ cup lemon juice
¾ cup honey
2-inch piece ginger root, sliced

1. Combine all the ingredients in a 2-quart or smaller slow cooker.

2. Cover and cook on high for 2–3 hours (if mixture begins to boil, turn heat to low).

3. Turn heat to low to keep warm for serving, or chill and serve over ice.

PER SERVING: Calories: 135 | Fat: 0g | Protein: 0g | Sodium: 14mg | Fiber: 0g | Carbohydrates: 37g | Sugar: 36g

Orange Juice

A thirst-quenching breakfast beverage, and an old-fashioned favorite.

INGREDIENTS | SERVES 6 (1-CUP SERVINGS)

5 cups water
Juice of 5 oranges
¾ cup honey
2-inch piece ginger root, sliced

1. Combine all the ingredients in a 2-quart slow cooker.

2. Cover and cook on high for 2–3 hours (if mixture begins to boil, turn heat to low).

3. Allow to cool and serve chilled.

PER SERVING: Calories: 180 | Fat: 0g | Protein: 1g | Sodium: 8mg | Fiber: 3g | Carbohydrates: 48g | Sugar: 45g

Candied Butternut Squash

Butternut squash has a delicious natural sweetness and is an excellent replacement for sweet potatoes. Also, you can now buy ready-cut and peeled butternut squash in many grocery stores (in the produce section), making this recipe incredibly easy to assemble.

INGREDIENTS | SERVES 4

4–5 cups cubed butternut squash

⅓ cup honey

1 tablespoon orange zest

½ teaspoon ground cinnamon

½ teaspoon ground cloves

Add all the ingredients to a greased 4-quart slow cooker. Cook on high for 3–4 hours or on low for 6–8 hours, until squash is fork-tender.

PER SERVING: Calories: 168 | Fat: 0g | Protein: 2g | Sodium: 9mg | Fiber: 4g | Carbohydrates: 44g | Sugar: 27g

Butternut Squash Versus Sweet Potatoes

Wondering which might be better for you? Actually, both are extremely healthy choices. Per serving, sweet potatoes have more fiber than the squash, but one cup of butternut squash contains fewer calories and fewer total carbohydrates. Both are high in vitamins A and C. In many recipes, they can be used interchangeably.

Saucy Brown "Sugar" Chicken

*Kids will love the sweet and sour flavors of honey and Dijon mustard in this
super-simple slow-cooker chicken. Serve chicken over butternut squash or alongside
a slow-cooked, baked, or steamed and mashed sweet potato.*

INGREDIENTS | SERVES 4

4 skinless, boneless chicken breasts
1 (12-ounce) jar peach salsa
¼ cup honey
1 tablespoon Dijon mustard

Slow Cooker Sundays

If you have multiple slow cookers, you can
make several main dishes at one time on
Sunday afternoons. The ready-made meals
can then be stored in the refrigerator for
up to 5 days or frozen. You will save money
and time by having homemade slow-
cooked meals already prepared.

1. Place chicken breasts in a greased 4-quart slow cooker.

2. In a small bowl, mix together the salsa, honey, and mustard. Pour over chicken in the slow cooker.

3. Cook on high for 3–4 hours or on low for 6–8 hours.

PER SERVING: Calories: 336 | Fat: 6g | Protein: 50g |
Sodium: 319mg | Fiber: 0g | Carbohydrates: 18g | Sugar: 17g

"French Fry" Casserole

A kid favorite that the whole family will love. Frozen sweet potato fries, ground beef, and a simple slow-cooked, Paleo-approved cream sauce make a tasty weeknight meal. Serve with a salad or steamed green beans.

INGREDIENTS | SERVES 4

1 pound ground beef
1 tablespoon coconut butter
½ onion, finely diced
1 cup mushrooms, sliced
½ green pepper, diced
2 tablespoons arrowroot powder
1⅓ cups (full-fat) coconut milk
½ teaspoon pepper
3 cups frozen sweet potato fries (shoestring cut)

Paleo Shortcuts

You can make several batches of Paleo-approved cream sauce at the beginning of the week to make meals even easier to put together. Simply make a batch, pour in a glass jar with an airtight lid, and store in the refrigerator for up to 1 week.

1. Brown ground beef in a skillet over medium heat for approximately 3–5 minutes. Pour cooked ground beef into a greased 2½-quart or larger slow cooker.

2. In a medium saucepan, melt the coconut butter. Add the onion, mushrooms, and green pepper. Cook for 3–5 minutes, until softened.

3. Mix the arrowroot powder with the coconut milk and slowly add to cooked vegetables. Whisk together for 5–10 minutes over medium heat until thickened.

4. Pour the cream sauce over the ground beef in the slow cooker. Sprinkle with pepper.

5. Top casserole with sweet potato fries. Vent the lid of the slow cooker with a chopstick to prevent extra condensation on the fries. Cook on high for 3–4 hours or on low for 5–6 hours.

PER SERVING: Calories: 224 | Fat: 11g | Protein: 23g | Sodium: 76mg | Fiber: 1g | Carbohydrates: 6g | Sugar: 1g

Gingerbread Pudding Cake

This somewhat messy concoction is a guaranteed kid-friendly favorite.

INGREDIENTS | SERVES 6

Nonstick cooking spray
½ cup almond flour
½ cup arrowroot powder
1 cup honey, divided
1 teaspoon baking powder
¼ teaspoon baking soda
1¼ teaspoons ground ginger
½ teaspoon ground cinnamon
¾ cup coconut milk
1 egg
½ cup raisins
2¼ cups water
½ cup coconut butter

1. Grease a 4-quart slow cooker with nonstick cooking spray.

2. In a medium bowl, whisk together the almond flour, arrowroot powder, ½ cup honey, baking powder, baking soda, ginger, and cinnamon.

3. Stir coconut milk and egg into the dry ingredients. Stir in raisins (batter will be thick). Spread gingerbread batter evenly in the bottom of the prepared slow cooker.

4. In a medium saucepan, combine the water, remaining ½ cup honey, and coconut butter. Bring to a boil; reduce heat. Boil gently, uncovered, for 2 minutes. Carefully pour water/honey mixture over the gingerbread batter.

5. Cover and vent lid with chopstick or the end of a wooden spoon. Cook on high for 2–2½ hours, until cake is cooked through and a toothpick inserted about ½ inch into the cake comes out clean. (It may not look like it's all the way cooked through.)

6. Remove slow cooker insert from the cooker. Allow to cool for 45–60 minutes to allow "pudding" to set beneath the cake.

7. To serve, spoon warm cake into dessert dishes and spoon "pudding sauce" over the warm cake.

PER SERVING: Calories: 369 | Fat: 12g | Protein: 4g | Sodium: 156mg | Fiber: 2g | Carbohydrates: 69g | Sugar: 54g

Chapter 12

Ethnic Cuisine

Caribbean Chicken Curry

Traditional Jamaican curries are cooked for long periods of time over the stove top, making them a logical fit for the slow cooker. The spices meld together and the chicken is meltingly tender.

INGREDIENTS | SERVES 8

1 tablespoon Madras curry powder

1 teaspoon allspice

½ teaspoon ground cloves

½ teaspoon ground nutmeg

1 teaspoon ground ginger

2 pounds boneless, skinless chicken thighs, cubed

1 teaspoon canola oil

1 large onion, chopped

2 cloves garlic, chopped

2 jalapeño peppers, chopped

⅓ cup light coconut milk

1. In a medium bowl, whisk together the curry powder, allspice, cloves, nutmeg, and ginger. Add the chicken and toss to coat each piece evenly.

2. Place the chicken in a nonstick skillet and quickly sauté for about 5–7 minutes, until the chicken starts to brown. Add to a 4-quart slow cooker along with the remaining spice mixture.

3. Heat the oil in a nonstick skillet and sauté the onion, garlic, and peppers for about 5–7 minutes, until fragrant. Add to the slow cooker.

4. Add the coconut milk to the slow cooker. Stir. Cook on low for 7–8 hours.

PER SERVING: Calories: 167 | Fat: 7g | Protein: 22g | Sodium: 99mg | Fiber: 1g | Carbohydrates: 2g | Sugar: 1g

Italian Chicken

This tastefully simple Italian favorite calls for just six ingredients.

INGREDIENTS | SERVES 6

6–8 boneless, skinless chicken breast tenderloins

2 bay leaves

½ teaspoon freshly ground black pepper

½ teaspoon dried oregano

½ teaspoon dried basil

32 ounces jarred or homemade tomato sauce

1. Add chicken to the bottom of a 4-quart slow cooker and sprinkle seasonings over chicken.

2. Pour sauce over seasoned chicken. Cover the chicken completely with sauce.

3. Cover and cook on low for 6 hours or on high for 3½–4 hours. Serve with an Italian vegetable medley.

PER SERVING: Calories: 395 | Fat: 8g | Protein: 69g | Sodium: 1,148mg | Fiber: 8g | Carbohydrates: 8g | Sugar: 6g

Greek Stew

This dish is loaded with fresh herbs and aromatic vegetables; it is just bursting with flavor.

INGREDIENTS | SERVES 10

3 tablespoons coconut oil

3 pounds grass-fed beef, cut into 1½-inch cubes

1 medium onion, chopped

10 large cloves garlic, lightly crushed

1 cup tomato purée (canned or fresh)

½ cup dry red wine

2 tablespoons lemon juice

2 bay leaves

1 cinnamon stick

4 whole cloves

Freshly ground black pepper, to taste

1 pound small pearl onions (optional)

2 tablespoons currants (optional)

1 cup walnut halves

1. In a Dutch oven, heat oil over medium-high heat, then brown the beef on all sides, about 5 minutes per side. Add the meat in batches, so the pot does not get overcrowded. Remove the meat and place in bowl so the juices are caught in the bowl.

2. Add the chopped onion and garlic cloves to the Dutch oven. Cook for about 4 minutes, stirring, until the onions are translucent.

3. Add the tomato purée, wine, and lemon juice to deglaze the Dutch oven.

4. Pour the meat and its juices back into the Dutch oven.

5. Add the bay leaves, cinnamon, and cloves, and season with pepper.

6. Place all the ingredients in a 4- or 6-quart slow cooker, and cook on high for 4 hours.

PER SERVING: Calories: 308 | Fat: 17g | Protein: 31g | Sodium: 174mg | Fiber: 1g | Carbohydrates: 5g | Sugar: 2g

Asian Pepper Steak

Serve with Asian vegetables like bok choy and Chinese cabbage.

INGREDIENTS | SERVES 4

2 pounds steak (sirloin is preferable, but any other good cut will do)

2 tablespoons coconut oil

Freshly ground black pepper, to taste

1–2 cloves garlic, minced

¼ cup wheat-free tamari

1 (16-ounce) can diced tomatoes

1 large green pepper, sliced into thin strips

1 small onion, sliced

1. On a chopping board, cut the steak on an angle to make strips about ½-inch thick.

2. In a large frying pan, add the oil and heat over medium heat. Sauté the steak for 10–15 minutes, until it lightly browns.

3. Drain excess fat, liberally coat the meat with ground pepper, and put the meat in a 4- or 6-quart slow cooker.

4. Add garlic and tamari, and mix so the steak is thoroughly coated. Cook on low for 6 hours.

5. One hour before serving, add tomatoes, green pepper, and onion. Cook on high for 1 hour and then serve piping hot.

PER SERVING: Calories: 383 | Fat: 16g | Protein: 49g | Sodium: 129mg | Fiber: 2g | Carbohydrates: 8g | Sugar: 5g

Creole Chicken

Top this recipe with some salsa to give it even more of a kick, and/or garnish with avocado slices.

INGREDIENTS | SERVES 4

4 skinless chicken breasts
Freshly ground black pepper, to taste
Cajun seasoning, to taste
1 (14½-ounce) can stewed, chopped
  tomatoes
1 stalk celery, diced
1 green pepper, diced
3 cloves garlic, minced
1 large onion, minced
4 ounces fresh mushrooms
1 fresh green chili, seeded and chopped

1. Place chicken in a 4-quart slow cooker. Season with pepper and Cajun seasoning.

2. Stir in the tomatoes, celery, green pepper, garlic, onion, mushrooms, and green chili.

3. Cook on low for 10–12 hours or on high for 5–6 hours.

PER SERVING: Calories: 302 | Fat: 6g | Protein: 52g | Sodium: 286mg | Fiber: 2g | Carbohydrates: 7g | Sugar: 3g

German Coleslaw

Serve with some slow-cooked chicken salad or seafood. Red or yellow peppers could be substituted here for the green peppers to give it a bit more color, like confetti!

INGREDIENTS | SERVES 4

1 teaspoon celery seeds
1½ cups lime juice
1½ teaspoons mustard seeds
1 teaspoon turmeric
1 teaspoon lemon juice
8 cups shredded cabbage
2 green peppers, finely chopped
1 large onion, finely chopped

1. In a saucepan over high heat, bring the celery seeds, lime juice, mustard seeds, turmeric, and lemon juice to a boil.

2. Place all vegetables into a 2-quart or smaller slow cooker.

3. Pour boiling liquid over vegetables. Cover and let stand, without heat, for 2 hours. Will keep crisp for 3–4 weeks in refrigerator.

PER SERVING: Calories: 70 | Fat: 1g | Protein: 3g | Sodium: 30mg | Fiber: 5g | Carbohydrates: 15g | Sugar: 8g

Ethiopian Chicken Stew

The eggs increase the protein, vitamin E, and omega-3 content of this recipe.

INGREDIENTS | SERVES 8

1 (14½-ounce) can diced tomatoes, with liquid

1½ pounds boneless, skinless chicken thighs

¼ cup lemon juice

2 tablespoons coconut butter

3 large onions, diced

1 tablespoon paprika

1 teaspoon ground ginger

1 teaspoon cayenne pepper

1 teaspoon turmeric

½ teaspoon freshly ground black pepper

2 cups water

8 hard-boiled eggs

1. Place tomatoes into a 6-quart slow cooker. Add the chicken thighs and lemon juice. Add the coconut butter, onions, and all the spices.

2. Add the water. Cover and cook on low for 6–8 hours or on high for 4–5 hours.

3. Ladle into bowls with a peeled hard-boiled egg in each individual bowl.

PER SERVING: Calories: 210 | Fat: 9g | Protein: 24g | Sodium: 151mg | Fiber: 2g | Carbohydrates: 9g | Sugar: 4g

"Jamaica-Me" Some Salmon

This Caribbean-themed favorite is a guaranteed hit. The variety of herbs and spices leave it exploding with flavor.

INGREDIENTS | SERVES 2

1 teaspoon onion powder

½ teaspoon ground cinnamon

¼ teaspoon freshly ground black pepper

¼ teaspoon ground chipotle chile pepper

⅛ teaspoon ground nutmeg

⅛ teaspoon ground ginger

⅛ teaspoon ground cloves

⅛ teaspoon dried thyme

2 teaspoons honey

1 teaspoon lemon juice

1 pound salmon

1. Combine the spices, thyme, honey, and lemon juice in a bowl.

2. Place the salmon on aluminum foil and rub (or brush) both sides of salmon with ingredients from the bowl. Fold over the foil and connect the sides, making a pocket. Fold sides to prevent fluids from leaking out from foil, and place pocket in a 6-quart slow cooker.

3. Cover and cook on low for 2 hours. When done, salmon should flake easily with a fork.

PER SERVING: Calories: 348 | Fat: 14g | Protein: 45g | Sodium: 100mg | Fiber: 1g | Carbohydrates: 8g | Sugar: 6g

Indian Lamb Curry

Lamb is a rich source of iron and zinc, as well as an excellent source of protein.

INGREDIENTS | SERVES 6

⅓ cup canola oil

3 medium yellow onions, chopped

4 cloves garlic, peeled and minced

1 (2-inch) piece ginger, peeled and grated

2 teaspoons cumin

1½ teaspoons cayenne pepper

1½ teaspoons turmeric

2 cups Beef Stock (page 79)

3 pounds boneless leg of lamb, cut into 1-inch cubes

6 cups baby spinach

1⅓ cups coconut milk

1. In a large frying pan over medium-high heat, warm the oil. Add onions and garlic, and sauté until golden, about 5 minutes.

2. Stir in the ginger, cumin, cayenne, and turmeric, and sauté until fragrant, about 30 seconds.

3. Pour in stock, raise heat to high, and deglaze the pan, stirring to scrape up the browned bits on the bottom. When broth comes to a boil, remove pan from heat.

4. Put lamb in a 4 or 6-quart slow cooker, and add contents of frying pan. Cover and cook on high for 4 hours or on low for 8 hours.

5. Add baby spinach to slow cooker and cook, stirring occasionally, until spinach is wilted, about 5 minutes.

6. Just before serving, stir in coconut milk. Spoon into shallow bowls and serve hot.

PER SERVING: Calories: 712 | Fat: 56g | Protein: 44g | Sodium: 162mg | Fiber: 2g | Carbohydrates: 9g | Sugar: 3g

Thai Curried Chicken

This chicken dish can be served wrapped in large lettuce leaves,
or over a Thai-themed vegetable medley.

INGREDIENTS | SERVES 8

2½ pounds boneless, skinless chicken breasts, cut into 1-inch cubes

½ cup Thai green curry paste

2¼ cups coconut milk

24 ounces broccoli florets

12 ounces cremini mushrooms, sliced

3 tablespoons fish sauce

½ cup honey

Juice of 1 lime

½ cup basil leaves, chopped

2 teaspoons almond meal

2 tablespoons water

1. In a 6-quart slow cooker, place the chicken, curry paste, and coconut milk. Stir to combine. Cover and cook on low for 4 hours.

2. Turn the cooker on high and add the broccoli and mushrooms.

3. In a separate bowl, whisk together the fish sauce, honey, and lime juice, and add this mixture to the slow cooker. Cover and cook for 30 minutes, then uncover and cook for 30 minutes more.

4. Stir in the basil.

5. In a separate bowl, whisk the almond meal with water, and add this mixture to the slow cooker. Stir, and cook for an additional 15–30 minutes, until the liquid has thickened slightly.

6. Serve hot, or rolled up in a lettuce leaf.

PER SERVING: Calories: 384 | Fat: 18g | Protein: 34g | Sodium: 200mg | Fiber: 3g | Carbohydrates: 26g | Sugar: 19g

Vietnamese Cucumber Soup

This is a simple, six-ingredient soup, easily prepared and ready in under three hours.

INGREDIENTS | SERVES 6

2 quarts water

1 pound ground pork, beef, chicken, or turkey

6 tablespoons fish sauce, divided

⅛ teaspoon freshly ground black pepper

4 large cucumbers, peeled, halved, de-seeded, and sliced

2 green onions, chopped

1. Get the water simmering in a large pot (to be placed inside a large slow cooker).

2. In a large bowl, combine the meat with 2 tablespoons of the fish sauce. Add the pepper and mix thoroughly.

3. Make meatballs out of the meat mixture and then transfer into boiling water, along with the cucumber slices. Cook for 15 minutes, and be sure to remove any foam and discard. Transfer the whole boiling pot into slow cooker.

4. Add the green onions and 4 remaining tablespoons of fish sauce. Cover and cook on high for 1½–2 hours.

PER SERVING: Calories: 198 | Fat: 16g | Protein: 13g | Sodium: 52mg | Fiber: 0g | Carbohydrates: 0g | Sugar: 0g

Amish Apple Butter

Traditionally flavored with warm spices and sweetened with honey, this condiment is called a "butter" due to its thick consistency and soft texture. Since apple butter needs a long, unhurried cooking period to caramelize the fruit and deepen the flavors, the slow cooker is the most suitable modern cooking appliance in which to make it.

INGREDIENTS | YIELDS 8 CUPS

10 cups (about 5 pounds) Gala apples, peeled, cored, and quartered

1 cup honey

3 tablespoons lemon juice

1½ teaspoons ground cinnamon

½ teaspoon ground cloves

½ teaspoon allspice

Old-Fashioned Apple Butter Making

Apple butter used to be made in large copper pots while simmering over a hot fire all day long. It was often done by a church group, or a large family who could share the responsibility of stirring the pot throughout the long day to prevent it from burning. Once finished, the apple butter would be canned and sold to raise money for a good cause or shared among all who helped make it.

1. Place the apples in a greased 4-quart slow cooker.

2. Pour honey and lemon juice over the apples and add cinnamon, cloves, and allspice. Stir to coat apples.

3. Cover and cook on low for 14–16 hours, until the apple butter is a deep, dark brown and is richly flavored.

4. Ladle into pint jars and store in the refrigerator for up to 6 weeks. You can also process and can the apple butter if you prefer.

PER SERVING: Calories: 132 | Fat: 0g | Protein: 0g | Sodium: 3mg | Fiber: 0g | Carbohydrates: 36g | Sugar: 35g

African Soup

Feel free to play around with the seasonings in this unique soup.
A small pinch of curry powder would be an excellent addition.

INGREDIENTS | SERVES 6

2 tablespoons olive oil

2 medium onions, chopped

2 large red bell peppers, seeded and chopped

4 cloves garlic, minced

1 (28-ounce) can crushed tomatoes

8 cups Roasted Vegetable Stock (page 79)

¼ teaspoon freshly ground black pepper

¼ teaspoon chili powder

⅔ cup natural almond or cashew butter

½ cup fresh chopped cilantro

Nut Allergies and Intolerances

Nut allergies are very serious and can be life threatening. If you have a child or family member who has nut allergies, use sunflower butter in this recipe instead.

1. Heat olive oil in a large skillet. Cook onions and bell peppers until softened, about 3–4 minutes.

2. Add garlic and cook for 1 minute more, stirring constantly. Add cooked vegetables to a greased 6-quart slow cooker.

3. Add tomatoes and their liquid, stock, black pepper, and chili powder to the slow cooker. Cover and cook on high for 4 hours or on low for 8 hours.

4. One hour prior to serving, stir in the almond butter. Heat for an additional 45–60 minutes, until soup has been completely warmed through. Garnish with cilantro.

PER SERVING: Calories: 154 | Fat: 5g | Protein: 3g | Sodium: 245mg | Fiber: 7g | Carbohydrates: 26g | Sugar: 15g

Greek Lemon-Chicken Soup

Lemon juice and egg yolks make this soup a lovely yellow color.
It's a unique soup that's perfect for a spring luncheon.

INGREDIENTS | SERVES 4

4 cups Chicken Stock (page 78)
¼ cup fresh lemon juice
¼ cup shredded carrots
¼ cup chopped onion
¼ cup chopped celery
⅛ teaspoon ground white pepper
2 tablespoons canola oil
2 tablespoons almond flour
4 egg yolks
½ cup diced, cooked boneless chicken breast
8 slices lemon

1. In a greased 4-quart slow cooker, combine the chicken stock, lemon juice, carrots, onion, celery, and pepper. Cover and cook on high for 3–4 hours or on low for 6–8 hours.

2. One hour before serving, blend the oil and the flour together in a medium bowl with a fork. Remove 1 cup of hot broth from the slow cooker and whisk with the oil and flour. Add mixture back to the slow cooker.

3. In a small bowl, beat the egg yolks until light in color. Gradually add some of the hot soup to the egg yolks, stirring constantly. Return the broth/egg mixture to the slow cooker.

4. Add the cooked chicken. Cook on low for an additional hour. Ladle hot soup into bowls and garnish with lemon slices.

PER SERVING: Calories: 181 | Fat: 14g | Protein: 6g | Sodium: 43mg | Fiber: 2g | Carbohydrates: 9g | Sugar: 3g

Mediterranean Chicken Casserole

Raisins may seem like an odd ingredient to add to a main dish, but they provide a slightly sweet flavor that beautifully complements the tomatoes and spices.

INGREDIENTS | SERVES 4

1 medium butternut squash, peeled and cut into 2-inch cubes

1 medium bell pepper, seeded and diced

1 (14½-ounce) can diced tomatoes, with liquid

4 boneless, skinless chicken breast halves, cut into bite-sized pieces

½ cup mild salsa

¼ cup raisins

¼ teaspoon ground cinnamon

¼ teaspoon ground cumin

¼ cup chopped fresh parsley

1. Add the squash and bell pepper to the bottom of a greased 4-quart slow cooker.

2. Mix the tomatoes, chicken, salsa, raisins, cinnamon, and cumin together and pour on top of squash and peppers.

3. Cover and cook on low for 6 hours or on high for 3 hours, until squash is fork-tender.

4. Remove the chicken and vegetables from slow cooker with slotted spoon. Ladle remaining sauce from slow cooker over the vegetables and chicken. Garnish with parsley.

PER SERVING: Calories: 189 | Fat: 3g | Protein: 26g | Sodium: 331mg | Fiber: 3g | Carbohydrates: 15g | Sugar: 10g

Asian-Inspired Honey-Glazed Chicken Drumsticks

It can be a challenge to eat at Chinese restaurants when you are abiding by the Paleolithic lifestyle. But this Asian-inspired chicken is a great substitute for take-out! Serve with a salad and egg drop soup.

INGREDIENTS | SERVES 4

2 pounds chicken drumsticks

1 tablespoon melted coconut butter

¼ cup lemon juice

¾ cup honey

1 teaspoon sesame oil

3 cloves garlic, crushed

½ teaspoon ground ginger

Sesame Oil

Sesame oil is a highly flavorful oil made from pressing either toasted or plain sesame seeds. It provides a unique nutty and earthy flavor to savory dishes. A little goes a long way, and it's not very expensive. It can be found at most grocery stores in the Asian food aisle.

1. Place the chicken drumsticks in a greased 4-quart slow cooker.

2. In a glass measuring cup, whisk together the melted butter, lemon juice, honey, sesame oil, garlic, and ginger.

3. Pour the honey sauce over the drumsticks. Cook on high for 3–4 hours or on low for 6–8 hours.

PER SERVING: Calories: 571 | Fat: 21g | Protein: 44g | Sodium: 192mg | Fiber: 0g | Carbohydrates: 54g | Sugar: 53g

Moroccan Chicken

This dish was inspired by traditional North African tagines (stews) and adapted for the slow cooker. Serve over mashed sweet potatoes.

INGREDIENTS | SERVES 6

½ teaspoon coriander

½ teaspoon cinnamon

1 teaspoon cumin

3 pounds (about 8) boneless, skinless chicken thighs, diced

1 large onion, thinly sliced

4 cloves garlic, minced

2 tablespoons minced fresh ginger or ½ teaspoon dried ginger

½ cup water

4 ounces dried apricots, halved

1. In a large bowl, combine the coriander, cinnamon, and cumin. Toss chicken in the spice mixture.

2. Place onion, garlic, ginger, and water into a 4-quart slow cooker. Place chicken on top of vegetables. Place dried apricots on top of chicken.

3. Cover and cook on low for 5–6 hours.

PER SERVING: Calories: 326 | Fat: 9g | Protein: 45g | Sodium: 197mg | Fiber: 2g | Carbohydrates: 15g | Sugar: 11g

Swiss Steak

Minute steaks are usually tenderized pieces of round steak. You can instead buy 2½ pounds of round steak, trim it of fat, cut it into six portions, and pound each portion thin between two pieces of plastic wrap. Serve Swiss Steak over mashed root vegetables.

INGREDIENTS | SERVES 6

½ cup almond flour
¼ teaspoon freshly ground black pepper
6 (6-ounce) beef minute steaks
2 tablespoons canola oil
2 teaspoons coconut butter
½ stalk celery, finely diced
1 large yellow onion, peeled and diced
1 cup beef broth
1 cup water
1 (1-pound) bag baby carrots

1. Add the almond flour, pepper, and steaks to a gallon-sized plastic bag; seal and shake to coat the meat.

2. Add the oil and coconut butter to a large skillet and bring it to temperature over medium-high heat. Add the meat and brown it for 5 minutes on each side. Transfer the meat to a 4-quart slow cooker.

3. Add the celery to the skillet and sauté while you add the onion to the plastic bag; seal and shake to coat the onion in flour. Add the flour-coated onion to the skillet and sauté for 10 minutes, stirring constantly, until the onions are lightly browned.

4. Add the broth to the skillet and stir to scrape up any browned bits clinging to the pan. Add the water and continue to cook until the liquid is thickened enough to lightly coat the back of a spoon. Pour into the slow cooker.

5. Add the carrots. Cover and cook on low for 8 hours.

6. Transfer the meat and carrots to a serving platter. Taste the gravy for seasoning, and add more pepper if desired. Serve alongside or over the meat and carrots.

PER SERVING: Calories: 392 | Fat: 22g | Protein: 39g | Sodium: 284mg | Fiber: 4g | Carbohydrates: 11g | Sugar: 5g

Mexican Pork Roast

Serve this pork over Mexican-themed vegetables, or as
Paleo-friendly "burritos" wrapped in lettuce leaves.

INGREDIENTS | SERVES 4

1 tablespoon olive oil

1 large sweet onion, peeled and sliced

1 medium carrot, peeled and finely diced

1 jalapeño pepper, seeded and minced

1 clove garlic, peeled and minced

¼ teaspoon dried Mexican oregano

¼ teaspoon ground coriander

¼ teaspoon freshly ground black pepper

1 (3-pound) pork shoulder or butt roast

1 cup chicken broth

1. Add the olive oil, onion, carrot, and jalapeño to a 4- to 6-quart slow cooker. Stir to coat the vegetables in the oil. Cover and cook on high for 30 minutes, or until the onions are softened. Stir in the garlic.

2. In a small bowl, combine the oregano, coriander, and black pepper. Rub the spice mixture onto the pork roast.

3. Add the rubbed pork roast to the slow cooker. Add the chicken broth. Cover and cook on low for 6 hours or until the pork is tender and pulls apart easily.

4. Use a slotted spoon to remove the pork and vegetables to a serving platter. Cover and let rest for 10 minutes.

5. Increase the temperature of the slow cooker to high. Cook for about 10–20 minutes, until the pan juices are reduced by half.

6. Use two forks to shred the pork and mix it in with the cooked onion and jalapeño. Ladle the reduced pan juices over the pork.

PER SERVING: Calories: 576 | Fat: 28g | Protein: 68g | Sodium: 530mg | Fiber: 1g | Carbohydrates: 8g | Sugar: 2g

Tuscan Chicken and Turkey Stew

You don't need a lot of ingredients to create a stew full of hearty and warm Tuscan flavors.

INGREDIENTS | SERVES 4

1 pound boneless, skinless chicken thighs

8 ounces ground turkey

1 (26-ounce) jar pasta sauce

1 can green beans, drained

1 teaspoon dried oregano

Change It Up

Don't like green beans or don't have them available in your pantry? Try this recipe with different vegetable combinations like mushrooms or artichokes.

1. Cut chicken thighs into bite-sized pieces. Place chicken into a greased 4-quart slow cooker.

2. Add the remaining ingredients. Stir to combine, and cook on high for 4 hours or on low for 8 hours.

PER SERVING: Calories: 391 | Fat: 14g | Protein: 36g | Sodium: 1,067mg | Fiber: 6g | Carbohydrates: 28g | Sugar: 17g

Chapter 13

Foods for Optimal Performance and Enhanced Recovery

Italian Tomato Sauce with Turkey Meatballs

Using roasted garlic eliminates the need for sautéing, making this recipe a snap to put together. Serve with Paleo "Pasta" (page 178) as a pregame meal.

INGREDIENTS | SERVES 4

12 ounces frozen turkey meatballs

1½ tablespoons minced basil

1 medium onion, minced

1 head roasted garlic (about 2 tablespoons), peels removed

1 (28-ounce) can fire-roasted tomatoes

1 teaspoon red pepper flakes

Defrost the meatballs according to package instructions. Place in a 4-quart slow cooker with the remaining ingredients. Stir. Cook on low for 3–6 hours. Stir before serving.

PER SERVING: Calories: 138 | Fat: 7g | Protein: 15g | Sodium: 80mg | Fiber: 1g | Carbohydrates: 3g | Sugar: 1g

Sweet Potato Soup

As a post-competition or training snack, this soup provides both fluid and carbohydrates to help refuel and rehydrate.

INGREDIENTS | SERVES 4

3 sweet potatoes, peeled and cubed

2 cups Chicken or Roasted Vegetable Stock (page 78 or 79)

1 (15-ounce) can sliced mangoes, undrained

¼ teaspoon ground allspice

½ cup coconut milk

1. Place all ingredients except coconut milk in a 4-quart slow cooker. Cover and cook on low for 8 hours or on high for 4 hours.

2. When sweet potatoes are soft, blend in blender and stir in coconut milk.

PER SERVING: Calories: 155 | Fat: 7g | Protein: 3g | Sodium: 67mg | Fiber: 4g | Carbohydrates: 22g | Sugar: 5g

Paleo Meatballs and Sauce

These meatballs are so close to the original, you won't know the difference. This recipe can also be served with Paleo "Pasta" (page 178) before or after competition to either fuel or refuel.

INGREDIENTS | YIELDS 12 MEATBALLS

1 (16-ounce) can diced, no-salt-added tomatoes

1 (4-ounce) can organic, no-salt-added tomato paste

2 pounds grass-fed ground beef

1 cup chopped celery

1 cup chopped onion

1 cup chopped carrots

4 cloves garlic, finely chopped

3 eggs

½ cup flaxseed meal

1 tablespoon oregano

1 teaspoon freshly ground black pepper

¼ teaspoon chili powder

1. Pour canned tomatoes and tomato paste into a 4-quart slow cooker.

2. Place all remaining ingredients in a large bowl and mix well with clean hands.

3. Roll resulting meat mixture into 2–3 ounce (large, rounded tablespoon) balls and add to slow cooker.

4. Cook on low for 5 hours minimum.

PER SERVING: (1 meatball) | Calories: 134 | Fat: 5g | Protein: 18g | Sodium: 82mg | Fiber: 1g | Carbohydrates: 3g | Sugar: 1g

Sweet Potatoes with an Orange Twist

This delicious dish gives you a sweet helping of performance fuel.

INGREDIENTS | SERVES 4

2 pounds sweet potatoes, peeled and cubed

½ cup honey

½ cup coconut butter

1 teaspoon vanilla extract

1 teaspoon ground cinnamon

½ teaspoon ground nutmeg

Juice of 1 medium orange

½ cup toasted chopped pecans

1. Place sweet potatoes in bottom of a 4- or 6-quart slow cooker.

2. Mix honey, coconut butter, vanilla, spices, and orange juice together. Stir into sweet potatoes. Cook on high for 2 hours or on low for 4 hours.

3. Stir in toasted pecans prior to serving.

PER SERVING: Calories: 422 | Fat: 10g | Protein: 5g | Sodium: 125mg | Fiber: 8g | Carbohydrates: 83g | Sugar: 45g

Sweet Potato Casserole

Inspired by Lauren, an aspiring field hockey player and fitness guru, this recipe is loaded with carbohydrates, and is a rich source of lots of beneficial vitamins and minerals. A great way to recharge after a long, hard workout.

INGREDIENTS | SERVES 6

2 pounds sweet potatoes, peeled and mashed

¼ cup canola oil

1⅓ cups honey, divided

1 tablespoon freshly squeezed orange juice

2 eggs, beaten

½ cup coconut milk

½ cup chopped pecans

2 tablespoons arrowroot powder

2 tablespoons coconut butter

1. Lightly grease a 4- or 6-quart slow cooker. Mix mashed sweet potatoes, canola oil, and ½ cup honey together in a large bowl.

2. Beat in orange juice, eggs, and coconut milk. Transfer to slow cooker.

3. In a medium bowl, combine the pecans, the remainder of the honey, arrowroot powder, and coconut butter. Spread evenly over the top of the sweet potatoes.

4. Cover and cook on high for 3–4 hours.

PER SERVING: Calories: 571 | Fat: 21g | Protein: 6g | Sodium: 111mg | Fiber: 6g | Carbohydrates: 96g | Sugar: 69g

Postgame Potent Pecans, Paleo Style

This recipe provides a blend of protein, fat, carbohydrates, calories, and even electrolytes to satisfy any athlete looking to recharge.

INGREDIENTS | SERVES 9

3 cups pecan halves

1 egg white

1 teaspoon cinnamon

¼ teaspoon cayenne pepper, or more to taste

1 cup honey

1. Place pecans in a 2-quart or smaller slow cooker, add egg white, and stir until evenly coated.

2. In a small bowl, stir the cinnamon, cayenne, and honey together and pour mixture over pecans, stirring until evenly coated.

3. Cover and cook on low for 3 hours, stirring every hour.

4. Uncover slow cooker, stir, and cook uncovered another 30–45 minutes, until pecans are dry. Cool and store in airtight container.

PER SERVING: Calories: 368 | Fat: 26g | Protein: 4g | Sodium: 8mg | Fiber: 4g | Carbohydrates: 36g | Sugar: 32g

Chicken and Sweet Potato Stew

*An easy way to meet pregame carbohydrate and fluids requirements,
and very low in fat to ensure optimal digestion.*

INGREDIENTS | SERVES 4

1 pound boneless, skinless chicken
breasts, cubed

12 ounces sweet potatoes, peeled and
cubed

12 ounces Chicken Stock (page 78)

1 large green bell pepper, sliced

2–3 teaspoons chili powder

½ teaspoon garlic powder

¼ cup cold water

2 tablespoons almond meal

Freshly ground black pepper, to taste

1. Combine all ingredients except water, almond meal, and pepper in a 4-quart slow cooker. Cover and cook on high for 4–5 hours.

2. In a small bowl, combine the almond meal and water. Add to the slow cooker, stirring 2–3 minutes. Season to taste with pepper.

PER SERVING: Calories: 247 | Fat: 5g | Protein: 27g |
Sodium: 205mg | Fiber: 5g | Carbohydrates: 22g | Sugar: 5g

Homemade Tomato Juice

Rehydrate and replenish. A perfect postexercise thirst quencher, loaded with electrolytes.

INGREDIENTS | SERVES 4

10 large tomatoes, seeded and sliced

1 teaspoon lemon juice

¼ teaspoon freshly ground black pepper

1 tablespoon honey

1. Place tomatoes in a 2-quart slow cooker. Cover and cook on low for 4–6 hours.

2. Press tomato mixture through a sieve. Add remaining ingredients and chill.

PER SERVING: Calories: 99 | Fat: 1g | Protein: 4g | Sodium: 23mg |
Fiber: 6g | Carbohydrates: 22g | Sugar: 16g

Sweet Potato Gratin with Leeks and Onions

The combination of sweet and savory makes this a fascinating, unique, and delicious dish.

INGREDIENTS | SERVES 6

2 leeks, white part only

2 large sweet onions, such as Vidalias, peeled and finely chopped

2 stalks celery with tops, finely chopped

4 tablespoons olive oil

Nonstick cooking spray

4 sweet potatoes, peeled and sliced thinly

1 teaspoon dried thyme

½ teaspoon freshly ground black pepper

3 cups coconut milk

1½ cups arrowroot powder

2 tablespoons coconut butter, cut in small pieces

1. In a skillet over medium heat, add the leeks, onions, celery, and olive oil. Sauté for 3–5 minutes, until softened.

2. Grease a 4-quart slow cooker with nonstick cooking spray.

3. Layer the sweet potato slices in the slow cooker with the sautéed vegetables. Sprinkle thyme and pepper on each layer as you go along. Finish with a layer of potatoes.

4. Add the coconut milk until it meets the top layer of potatoes. Then add the arrowroot powder. Dot with the coconut butter.

5. Cover and cook on high for 4 hours or on low for 8 hours, until the potatoes are fork-tender. In the last hour of cooking, vent the lid of the slow cooker with a chopstick or wooden spoon handle to allow excess condensation to escape.

PER SERVING: Calories: 530 | Fat: 33g | Protein: 5g | Sodium: 71mg | Fiber: 5g | Carbohydrates: 58g | Sugar: 7g

Beef and Sweet Potato Stew

*This rich, deeply flavored beef stew with sweet potatoes is inspired by Lara—
an aspiring young field hockey player who adheres to a strict gluten-free diet.*

INGREDIENTS | SERVES 8

¾ cup almond flour

1½ teaspoons lemon juice, divided

1½ teaspoons freshly ground black pepper, divided

1¼ pounds stew beef, cut into 1-inch chunks

¼ cup olive oil, divided

1 medium yellow onion, diced

2 cups peeled and diced carrots

¾ pound cremini mushrooms, cut in half

6 cloves garlic, minced

3 tablespoons tomato paste

1 pound sweet potatoes, peeled and diced

4½ cups Beef Stock (page 79)

1 bay leaf

1½ teaspoons dried thyme

1 tablespoon honey

1. In a large zip-top plastic bag, place flour, 1 teaspoon lemon juice, and 1 teaspoon pepper. Add beef and close the bag. Shake lightly, open bag, and make sure that all of the beef is coated in flour and seasoning. Set aside.

2. In a large skillet, heat 2 tablespoons olive oil over medium heat. Cook beef in small batches until browned on all sides, about 1 minute per side. Add beef to a greased 4- to 6-quart slow cooker.

3. In the same skillet, heat the remaining 2 tablespoons olive oil. Add onion and carrots, and cook until onions are translucent, about 5 minutes.

4. Add mushrooms and garlic, and cook for another 2–3 minutes.

5. Add tomato paste and heat through. De-glaze the pan, scraping the stuck-on bits from the bottom of the pan. Add cooked vegetable mixture on top of the beef in the slow cooker.

6. Add the sweet potatoes, stock, bay leaf, and thyme to the slow cooker. Cover and cook on low for 8 hours or on high for 4 hours.

7. Before serving, add honey and remaining lemon juice and pepper.

PER SERVING: Calories: 260 | Fat: 12g | Protein: 18g | Sodium: 578mg | Fiber: 3g | Carbohydrates: 20g | Sugar: 7g

Cabbage and Beef Casserole

A lower-carbohydrate beefy casserole using cabbage and tomato sauce.

INGREDIENTS | SERVES 6

2 pounds ground beef

1 small onion, chopped

1 head cabbage, shredded

1 (16-ounce) can tomatoes

½ teaspoon garlic powder

¼ teaspoon ground thyme

¼ teaspoon red pepper flakes

½ teaspoon oregano

8 ounces tomato sauce

1. In a large skillet, brown the ground beef for about 5–6 minutes. Remove ground beef to a bowl and set aside. In the same skillet, sauté onion until softened, about 3–5 minutes.

2. In a greased 4- to 6-quart slow cooker, layer cabbage, onion, tomatoes, garlic powder, thyme, pepper flakes, oregano, and beef. Repeat layers, ending with beef. Pour tomato sauce over casserole.

3. Cook on low for 8 hours or on high for 4 hours.

PER SERVING: Calories: 269 | Fat: 8g | Protein: 35g | Sodium: 429mg | Fiber: 5g | Carbohydrates: 15g | Sugar: 9g

Lamb and Root Vegetable Tagine

This exotic dish provides a rich source of long-lasting carbohydrates with the combination of dried fruit and root vegetables.

INGREDIENTS | SERVES 6

1 tablespoon olive oil

2 pounds leg of lamb, trimmed of fat and cut into bite-sized chunks

½ large onion, chopped

1 clove garlic, minced

½ teaspoon freshly ground black pepper

1 cup Chicken Stock (page 78)

½ pound (about 2 medium) sweet potatoes, peeled and cut into 1-inch chunks

⅓ cup dried apricots, cut in half

1 teaspoon coriander

1 teaspoon cumin

¼ teaspoon cinnamon

1. In a large skillet, brown the cubed lamb in olive oil, approximately 1–2 minutes per side. Add lamb to a greased 4-quart slow cooker.

2. Cook the onion and garlic in the same skillet for 3–4 minutes, until soft, and then add to the slow cooker.

3. Add remaining ingredients to slow cooker. Cook on high for 4 hours or on low for 8 hours.

PER SERVING: Calories: 393 | Fat: 24g | Protein: 29g | Sodium: 111mg | Fiber: 2g | Carbohydrates: 15g | Sugar: 6g

Orange Chicken

Serve this dish over stir-fry vegetables or a puréed starchy or root vegetable.

INGREDIENTS | SERVES 8

Nonstick cooking spray

3 pounds boneless, skinless chicken breasts

1 small onion, peeled and diced

½ cup freshly squeezed orange juice

3 tablespoons orange marmalade or Peach Marmalade (page 33)

1 tablespoon honey

1 tablespoon lemon juice

1 teaspoon Dijon mustard

1 tablespoon arrowroot powder mixed with 2 tablespoons hot water

2 tablespoons grated orange zest

1. Grease the slow cooker with nonstick cooking spray.

2. Cut the chicken breasts into bite-sized pieces. Add the chicken and the onion to the slow cooker.

3. In a small bowl, mix together the orange juice, marmalade, honey, lemon juice, and mustard. Pour over the chicken in the slow cooker.

4. Cover and cook on low for 5–6 hours or until chicken is cooked through.

5. About 10 minutes before serving, whisk in the arrowroot powder slurry. Leave the slow cooker uncovered, turn the temperature to high, and continue to cook for 10 minutes to thicken the sauce. Serve with orange zest sprinkled on top.

PER SERVING: Calories: 235 | Fat: 4g | Protein: 36g | Sodium: 208mg | Fiber: 0g | Carbohydrates: 11g | Sugar: 9g

Chicken and "Paleo-Approved" Dumplings

Fluffy Paleo dumplings float on top of a savory chicken stew.
The perfect combination of protein and energy-producing carbohydrates.

INGREDIENTS | SERVES 4

4 chicken breasts, cut into chunks

4 cups Chicken Stock (page 78)

1 teaspoon freshly ground black pepper

2 stalks celery, thinly sliced

2 large carrots, thinly sliced

½ large onion, finely chopped

1 cup almond flour

1 cup arrowroot starch

1 teaspoon xanthan gum

1 tablespoon honey

3 teaspoons baking powder

⅓ cup coconut butter

2 eggs, lightly beaten

1 cup coconut milk

1. Place the chicken in a greased 4- to 6-quart slow cooker. Add chicken stock, pepper, celery, carrots, and onion. Cook on high for 3–4 hours or on low for 6–8 hours.

2. In a mixing bowl, whisk together the flour, arrowroot starch, xanthan gum, honey, and baking powder.

3. Cut the coconut butter into the dry ingredients with two knives or a pastry cutter until the mixture resembles small peas. Make a well in the center of the dry ingredients and add the eggs and coconut milk. Gently mix the wet ingredients into the dry ingredients until you have a fluffy dough.

4. Thirty minutes before serving, carefully drop the dough in golf ball–sized spoonfuls into the hot chicken broth. Place the lid on the slow cooker and do not open it for 30 minutes so the dumplings will rise and cook through.

5. Serve dumplings with broth and chicken in large bowls.

PER SERVING: Calories: 658 | Fat: 33g | Protein: 47g | Sodium: 653mg | Fiber: 6g | Carbohydrates: 48g | Sugar: 8g

Turkey Meatballs with Tangy Apricot Sauce

These easy turkey meatballs obtain their flavor from the tasty sweet and sour combination.
An excellent and valuable pregame or postgame fuel (or refuel) source.

INGREDIENTS | SERVES 4

1 pound ground turkey

¾ cup almond flour

1 egg

¼ cup finely diced onions

¼ cup finely diced celery

½ teaspoon freshly ground black pepper

1 tablespoon olive oil

1 cup apricot preserves or Peach Marmalade (page 33)

¼ cup Dijon mustard

Are Meatballs Paleo-Approved?

Meatloaf and meatballs are usually made with wheat bread crumbs. To make meatloaf or meatballs Paleo-friendly, simply replace the bread crumbs called for in a recipe with almond flour and/or arrowroot powder.

1. In a large bowl, mix together the ground turkey, almond flour, egg, onions, celery, and ground pepper. Roll into small meatballs (about sixteen to twenty). The meatball mixture will be slightly wet.

2. Heat olive oil in a large skillet. Add meatballs to hot skillet and brown on all sides, about 1 minute per side.

3. Grease a 2½-quart slow cooker. Add browned meatballs to the slow cooker.

4. In a small bowl, mix together the preserves (or marmalade) and mustard. Pour the sauce over the meatballs. Cook on high for 3 hours or on low for 6 hours.

5. If using meatballs as an appetizer instead of a main course, you can turn the slow cooker to the warm setting and heat them for up to 2 hours.

PER SERVING: Calories: 350 | Fat: 25g | Protein: 26g | Sodium: 307mg | Fiber: 3g | Carbohydrates: 7g | Sugar: 2g

Apricot Pork Sirloin Roast

A pork sirloin roast is low in fat, yet it cooks up tender and moist. If you prefer gravy instead of sauce, simply mix the reduced pan juices with some full-fat coconut milk.

INGREDIENTS | SERVES 8

15 pitted prunes (dried plums)

12 dried apricots, pitted

½ cup boiling water

1 cup Chicken Stock (page 78)

1 cup apple juice

1 (3½-pound) pork sirloin roast, trimmed of fat and silver skin

4 large sweet potatoes, peeled and quartered

Freshly ground black pepper, to taste

1 tablespoon arrowroot powder

2 tablespoons cold water

1. Add the prunes and apricots to a 6-quart slow cooker. Pour the boiling water over the dried fruit; cover and let set for 15 minutes.

2. Add the chicken stock, apple juice, pork sirloin roast, sweet potatoes, and pepper. Cover and cook on low for 5–6 hours or until the internal temperature of the roast is 160°F.

3. Remove the meat and sweet potatoes from the cooker; cover and keep warm.

4. Turn the cooker to high. Use an immersion blender to purée the fruit.

5. In a small bowl, mix the arrowroot powder into the cold water. Once the liquid in the slow cooker begins to bubble around the edges, slowly whisk in the arrowroot liquid. Reduce the heat to low, and simmer the sauce for several minutes, stirring occasionally, until thickened.

6. Place the pork roast on a serving platter and carve into eight slices. Arrange the sweet potatoes around the pork. Ladle the sauce over the meat. Serve immediately.

PER SERVING: Calories: 398 | Fat: 7g | Protein: 46g | Sodium: 265mg | Fiber: 4g | Carbohydrates: 36g | Sugar: 17g

Roast Pork with Cinnamon Cranberries and Sweet Potatoes

You can substitute Peach Marmalade (page 33) for the orange marmalade and orange juice called for in this recipe. Doing so will add a subtle taste of peaches and pineapple to the dish, too.

INGREDIENTS | SERVES 6

1 (3-pound) pork butt roast

Freshly ground black pepper, to taste

1 (16-ounce) can sweetened whole cranberries

1 medium onion, peeled and diced

¼ cup orange marmalade

½ cup freshly squeezed orange juice

¼ teaspoon ground cinnamon

¼ teaspoon ground cloves

3 large sweet potatoes, peeled and quartered

1 tablespoon arrowroot powder (optional)

2 tablespoons cold water (optional)

1. Place the pork, fat side up, in a 4-quart slow cooker and add pepper to taste.

2. In a medium bowl, combine the cranberries, onion, marmalade, orange juice, cinnamon, and cloves, and stir to mix. Pour over the pork roast in the slow cooker.

3. Arrange the sweet potatoes around the meat. Cover and cook on low for 6 hours or until the pork is tender and pulls apart easily.

4. To serve with a thickened sauce, transfer the meat and sweet potatoes to a serving platter. Cover and keep warm. Skim any fat off of the pan juices. (You'll want about 2 cups of juice remaining in the cooker.) Cover and cook on high setting for 30 minutes, or until the pan liquids begin to bubble around the edges. In a small bowl, combine the arrowroot powder with the water. Whisk into the liquid in the slow cooker. Reduce temperature to low, and continue to cook and stir for an additional 2 minutes, or until it is thickened and bubbly.

PER SERVING: Calories: 390 | Fat: 8g | Protein: 52g | Sodium: 154mg | Fiber: 2g | Carbohydrates: 26g | Sugar: 12g

Sweet and Sour Shrimp with Pineapple

Serve over a generous portion of seasonal vegetable blend. Shrimp is a great source of high-quality protein, and combined with all the vegetables and simple sugars, this dish makes an excellent protein/carb combo; the perfect recipe for optimal recovery.

INGREDIENTS | SERVES 4

3 (8-ounce) cans pineapple chunks, drained and 1 cup juice reserved

2 (6-ounce) packages frozen green beans, thawed

¼ cup arrowroot powder

⅓ cup plus 2 teaspoons honey

2 cups Chicken Stock (page 78)

1 teaspoon ground ginger

1 pound medium or large shrimp, peeled and deveined

¼ cup lemon juice

1. Place pineapple and green beans in a 2- or 4-quart slow cooker.

2. In a medium saucepan, combine the arrowroot powder, honey, and chicken stock. Add 1 cup reserved pineapple juice and ginger.

3. Bring saucepan contents to a boil for 1 minute, and then pour into the slow cooker.

4. Cover and cook on low for 4½–5½ hours.

5. Add shrimp and lemon juice. Cover and cook on low for 30 minutes.

PER SERVING: Calories: 375 | Fat: 2g | Protein: 25g | Sodium: 177mg | Fiber: 5g | Carbohydrates: 68g | Sugar: 53g

Hawaiian Fruit Compote

A must-have pregame/training last-minute energizer.

INGREDIENTS | SERVES 6

3 cups pineapple, coarsely chopped

3 grapefruit, peeled and sectioned

3 cups chopped fresh peaches

3 limes, peeled and sectioned

1 mango, peeled and chopped

2 bananas, peeled and sliced

1 tablespoon lemon juice

1 (21-ounce) can cherry pie filling

Slivered almonds (optional)

1. Place all the ingredients except almonds in a 2-quart slow cooker. Mix well.

2. Cover and cook on low for 4–5 hours or on high for 2–3 hours.

3. Serve topped with almonds, if desired.

PER SERVING: Calories: 180 | Fat: 1g | Protein: 3g | Sodium: 3mg | Fiber: 6g | Carbohydrates: 47g | Sugar: 34g

Pear Slush

Fulfills the two most important post-workout needs: replenishes carbohydrate stores and rehydrates!

INGREDIENTS | SERVES 6

1 pound fresh pears, cored (Bosc are preferred)

1¼ cups water

¼ cup honey

½ teaspoon ground cinnamon

1 tablespoon lemon juice

Ice Fruit

Enjoy this deliciously cool, thirst-quenching treat as a postgame snack to cool down, or as a pregame energizer, for a last-minute burst of high-quality carbohydrates and fluids.

1. Place the pears, water, honey, and cinnamon in a 2-quart slow cooker. Cover and cook on high for 2½–3½ hours. Stir in the lemon juice.

2. Process pear and syrup mixture in a blender until smooth. Strain mixture through a sieve, and discard any pulp.

3. Pour liquid into an 11" × 9" baking dish, cover tightly with plastic wrap, and transfer to freezer.

4. Stir every hour with a fork, crushing any lumps as it freezes. Freeze 3–4 hours or until firm.

PER SERVING: Calories: 87 | Fat: 0g | Protein: 0g | Sodium: 3mg | Fiber: 2g | Carbohydrates: 23g | Sugar: 19g

Apple Freeze

Inspired by Buddy and his never-ending love for frozen applesauce.

INGREDIENTS | SERVES 6

1 pound fresh apples, cored (Golden Delicious are preferred)

1¼ cups water

¼ cup honey

½ teaspoon ground cinnamon

1 tablespoon lemon juice

1. Place the apples, water, honey, and cinnamon in 2-quart slow cooker. Cover and cook on high for 2½–3½ hours. Stir in the lemon juice.

2. Process apple and syrup mixture in a blender until smooth. Strain mixture through a sieve, and discard any pulp.

3. Pour liquid into an 11" × 9" baking dish, cover tightly with plastic wrap, and transfer to freezer.

4. Stir every hour with a fork, crushing any lumps as it freezes. Freeze 3–4 hours or until firm.

PER SERVING: Calories: 80 | Fat: 0g | Protein: 0g | Sodium: 3mg | Fiber: 1g | Carbohydrates: 21g | Sugar: 19g

Chapter 14

Stone Age Sweet Treats:
Slow-Cooked Desserts

"Baked" Apples

Serve these lightly spiced apples as a simple dessert or as a breakfast treat.

INGREDIENTS | SERVES 6

6 baking apples

½ cup water

1 cinnamon stick

1 knob peeled fresh ginger

1 vanilla bean

Baking with Apples

When baking or cooking, choose apples with firm flesh such as Granny Smith, Jonathan, McIntosh, Cortland, Pink Lady, Pippin, or Winesap. They will be able to hold up to long cooking times without turning to mush. Leaving the skin on adds fiber.

1. Place the apples in a single layer on the bottom of a 4- to 6-quart slow cooker. Add the water, cinnamon stick, ginger, and vanilla bean. Cook on low for 6–8 hours or until the apples are tender and easily pierced with a fork.

2. Use a slotted spoon to remove the apples from the insert. Discard the cinnamon stick, ginger, vanilla bean, and water. Serve hot.

PER SERVING: Calories: 77 | Fat: 0g | Protein: 0g | Sodium: 1mg | Fiber: 2g | Carbohydrates: 21g | Sugar: 16g

Slow-Cooked Pineapple

Slow cooking makes pineapple meltingly tender.

INGREDIENTS | SERVES 8

1 whole pineapple, peeled

1 vanilla bean, split

3 tablespoons water or rum

Cooking with Vanilla Beans

Vanilla beans have a natural "seam" that can easily be split to release the flavorful seeds inside. After using a vanilla bean, wash it and allow it to dry. Then place it in a container with a few cups of sugar for a few weeks to make vanilla sugar.

Place all ingredients into a 4-quart oval slow cooker. Cook on low for 4 hours or until fork-tender. Remove the vanilla bean before serving.

PER SERVING: Calories: 57 | Fat: 0g | Protein: 1g | Sodium: 1mg | Fiber: 2g | Carbohydrates: 15g | Sugar: 11g

Paleo Brownie Bowls

Whoever said brownies were "Paleo No" foods? Perish the thought!

INGREDIENTS | SERVES 2

½ cup almond butter

¼ cup honey

⅛ cup cocoa powder

1 teaspoon vanilla extract

1 egg

¼ teaspoon baking soda

Dash pumpkin pie spice

Dash ground ginger (optional)

2 ceramic coffee mugs

Coconut oil, for greasing

1. Combine all the ingredients in a large mixing bowl and mix well. Grease coffee mugs with some coconut oil, so your brownie doesn't get stuck all over the sides of the mug.

2. Pour even amounts of the batter into mugs, and set them inside a 4-quart slow cooker. Don't fill the mugs any more than about halfway full; the batter will rise and bubble over if mugs are too full.

3. Cover and cook on high for about 1½–2 hours, depending on desired cake-like consistency. Knife inserted into center of brownie should come out mostly clean.

4. Remove lid and allow to cool before serving.

PER SERVING: Calories: 183 | Fat: 3g | Protein: 4g | Sodium: 195mg | Fiber: 2g | Carbohydrates: 38g | Sugar: 35g

Warm Spiced Fruit

*This recipe can be used with a variety of different fruits. Serve as dessert or as
a sweet addition to a slow-cooked breakfast, brunch, or dinner dish of choice.*

INGREDIENTS | SERVES 8

1 (28-ounce) can peach slices, drained

1 (16-ounce) can pineapple tidbits with
natural juices, undrained

1 (28-ounce) can pear slices, drained

1 (15-ounce) can mixed chunky fruit

½ cup maraschino cherries, drained

½ cup honey

4 tablespoons coconut butter

1 tablespoon almond meal

1½ teaspoons ground cinnamon

1 teaspoon ground nutmeg

1. Combine all the ingredients in a 4-quart slow cooker;
stir gently.

2. Cover and cook on low for 4–6 hours or on high for
2–3 hours.

PER SERVING: Calories: 257 | Fat: 1g | Protein: 1g |
Sodium: 15mg | Fiber: 6g | Carbohydrates: 66g | Sugar: 60g

Cranberry-Apple Compote

An easy, succulent taste of fall.

INGREDIENTS | SERVES 6

4 cups peeled, sliced apples

½ cup sliced cranberries

⅓ cup honey

2 tablespoons coconut oil

1 teaspoon ground cinnamon

¼ teaspoon ground nutmeg

¾ cup chopped walnuts and almonds

1. Combine all the ingredients except nuts in a 3- to 4-quart
slow cooker.

2. Cover and cook on high for 1½–2 hours or until apples
are tender.

3. Sprinkle each serving with nuts.

PER SERVING: Calories: 221 | Fat: 10g | Protein: 3g |
Sodium: 1mg | Fiber: 3g | Carbohydrates: 36g | Sugar: 30g

Sweet and Spicy Walnuts

A perfect sweet and savory snack, guaranteed to please just about any palate.

INGREDIENTS | SERVES 12

2 tablespoons coconut oil

¼ cup honey

1 teaspoon ground ginger

1 teaspoon curry powder

½ teaspoon cayenne pepper

¼ teaspoon onion powder

¼ teaspoon garlic powder

3 cups shelled walnuts

1. Pour coconut oil into a 2- to 4-quart slow cooker, turn on high, and allow to melt.

2. While oil is melting, in a separate bowl, mix honey and seasonings together.

3. Once oil is melted, add walnuts to slow cooker and stir. Add honey and seasoning blend to slow cooker, and stir until evenly coated.

4. Cover and cook on high for 1 hour. Stir the nuts, cover, and cook for another hour.

5. Remove cover and cook an additional 20–30 minutes, until the nuts are dry. Cool and store in airtight containers.

PER SERVING: Calories: 214 | Fat: 19g | Protein: 5g | Sodium: 1mg | Fiber: 2g | Carbohydrates: 10g | Sugar: 7g

Bananas Foster

Not just good . . . Heavenly. Words just cannot describe the level of deliciousness this recipe creates.

INGREDIENTS | SERVES 3

3 overripe bananas
4 tablespoons coconut butter
⅓ cup honey
1 teaspoon vanilla extract

1. Place bananas into a zip-top plastic bag, and mash.

2. Squeeze banana pulp into a 2-quart slow cooker. Add coconut butter, honey, and vanilla.

3. Cover and cook on low for 3–4 hours or on high for 1–2 hours.

PER SERVING: Calories: 224 | Fat: 0g | Protein: 1g | Sodium: 3mg | Fiber: 3g | Carbohydrates: 58g | Sugar: 46g

Vanilla-Infused Fruit Cocktail

Try this recipe with a different fruit combination each time.

INGREDIENTS | SERVES 8

16 ounces prunes, pitted
8 ounces dried apricots
8 ounces dried pears
3 cups water
½ cup honey
2 tablespoons fresh lemon juice
1 teaspoon finely grated lemon zest
½ vanilla bean or ½ teaspoon vanilla extract

1. Combine all the ingredients in a 4- to 6-quart slow cooker.

2. Cook on low for about 6–8 hours or until the fruit is tender.

3. Serve warm or at room temperature.

PER SERVING: Calories: 284 | Fat: 0g | Protein: 2g | Sodium: 9mg | Fiber: 7g | Carbohydrates: 75g | Sugar: 57g

Island-Inspired Fruit Crisp

An irresistible blend of tropical fruit and coconut flavors.

INGREDIENTS | SERVES 6

Nonstick cooking spray

2 (21-ounce) cans apricot pie filling

1 (7-ounce) package tropical blend mixed dried fruit bits

1 cup crushed almonds and walnuts

⅓ cup toasted coconut

How to Toast Coconut

Spread coconut flakes in a shallow baking pan and bake in a preheated oven at 350°F for 5–10 minutes, or until golden brown. Watch closely to avoid burning, and shake the pan once or twice while cooking.

1. Lightly coat the inside of a 3½- to 4-quart slow cooker with nonstick cooking spray.

2. Combine the pie filling and dried fruit bits in slow cooker.

3. Cover and cook on low for 2½ hours. Remove liner from cooker, if possible, or turn off cooker.

4. In a small bowl, combine the nuts and coconut. Sprinkle over fruit mixture in cooker.

5. Let stand, uncovered, for 30 minutes to cool slightly before serving.

6. To serve, spoon warm mixture into dessert dishes.

PER SERVING: Calories: 186 | Fat: 9g | Protein: 4g | Sodium: 7mg | Fiber: 5g | Carbohydrates: 25g | Sugar: 1g

Caveman "Choc" Pot

A Paleo-approved, delectable chocolate mousse-like dessert.

INGREDIENTS | SERVES 8

5 egg yolks
2 cups coconut milk
½ cup honey
1 tablespoon vanilla extract
¼ cup unsweetened cocoa powder

1. Place an oven-safe dish inside of a 6-quart slow cooker and add water around the dish, making a water bath. Fill water until it reaches the halfway point of the dish.

2. Whip egg yolks, coconut milk, honey, vanilla, and cocoa powder together and pour mixture into dish. Cook on high for 2–4 hours.

3. Unplug the slow cooker, let dish cool and remove from slow cooker. Keep in refrigerator for 2–3 hours before serving.

PER SERVING: Calories: 214 | Fat: 15g | Protein: 3g | Sodium: 13mg | Fiber: 0g | Carbohydrates: 20g | Sugar: 18g

Perfect Pear O' Sweetness

The attractive finished product makes for a great holiday dish.

INGREDIENTS | SERVES 8

8 firm ripe pears, peeled
½ cup sliced cranberries
¾ cup honey
¼ teaspoon ground ginger
¼ teaspoon ground cinnamon
⅛ teaspoon ground cloves
Juice of 1 lemon
2 tablespoons lime juice

1. Stand the pears upright in a 6-quart slow cooker. Sprinkle on the cranberries.

2. In a separate bowl, combine the honey, ginger, cinnamon, and cloves, and spoon on top of the pears. Pour the lemon and lime juice evenly over the contents.

3. Cover and cook on low for 4 hours or on high for 2 hours.

PER SERVING: Calories: 219 | Fat: 0g | Protein: 1g | Sodium: 3mg | Fiber: 6g | Carbohydrates: 59g | Sugar: 47g

Paleo Poached Peaches with Raspberry and Vanilla

This can be made with either Marsala wine or sherry.

INGREDIENTS | SERVES 6

⅔ cup Marsala wine

⅔ cup water

⅓ cup honey

6 firm, ripe peaches, pitted and halved

1 vanilla bean, slit lengthwise

2 teaspoons arrowroot powder

1 cup raspberries

1. Pour the wine, water, and honey into a saucepan and bring to a boil.

2. Place the peach halves and vanilla bean into 4- to 6-quart slow cooker, and pour on hot syrup from saucepan.

3. Cover and cook on low for 1–1½ hours or until hot and tender.

4. Remove peaches and vanilla bean. Scrape seeds from vanilla bean and return seeds back to cooking syrup in slow cooker.

5. Mix the arrowroot powder with about ½ teaspoon water to create a paste, and stir into syrup.

6. Cook on high for 15 minutes, stirring periodically. Pour thickened syrup over peaches, add the raspberries, and serve warm or chilled.

PER SERVING: Calories: 170 | Fat: 1g | Protein: 2g | Sodium: 4mg | Fiber: 4g | Carbohydrates: 36g | Sugar: 31

Chunky Apple-Cherry Sauce

Enjoy warm as a breakfast fruit, or chilled as a sweet summer treat.

INGREDIENTS | YIELDS 6 (½-CUP) SERVINGS

5 Golden Delicious apples, peeled, cored, and sliced

2 tablespoons water

¼ cup honey

½ cup cherry preserves

1. Place apple slices in a greased 4- to 6-quart slow cooker. Add water and honey, and toss to coat the apples. Cover and cook on low for 6–7 hours.

2. Stir in the cherry preserves.

3. Serve warm or allow to cool and serve chilled.

PER SERVING: (½ cup) | Calories: 118 | Fat: 0g | Protein: 0g | Sodium: 9mg | Fiber: 0g | Carbohydrates: 30g | Sugar: 25g

Pumpkin Pie Pudding

A flavorful, festive, and favorite holiday treat.

INGREDIENTS | SERVES 8

1 (15-ounce) can solid-pack pumpkin, softened

1 (12-ounce) can coconut milk

¾ cup honey

½ cup almond meal

2 eggs, beaten

2 tablespoons coconut butter, melted

2 tablespoons honey

2 teaspoons pumpkin pie spice

1 teaspoon coconut extract

Nonstick cooking spray

1. In a large bowl, stir together pumpkin and ¼ cup coconut milk, stirring until well blended with the pumpkin.

2. Add remaining coconut milk and the remaining ingredients, and beat until blended.

3. Transfer to a 3- to 4-quart slow cooker coated with nonstick cooking spray.

4. Cover and cook on low for 6–8 hours, until pudding is set when lightly touched with finger.

PER SERVING: Calories: 271 | Fat: 14g | Protein: 5g | Sodium: 27mg | Fiber: 2g | Carbohydrates: 38g | Sugar: 33g

Crustless Apple Pie

Adjust the cooking time depending on the type of apple you use. A softer Golden Delicious should be cooked through and soft in the recommended cooking times, but a crisper Granny Smith apple may take longer.

INGREDIENTS | SERVES 8

Nonstick cooking spray

8 medium apples, cored and sliced

3 tablespoons freshly squeezed orange juice

3 tablespoons water

½ cup pecans, chopped

⅓ cup honey

¼ cup coconut butter, melted

½ teaspoon cinnamon

1. Grease the slow cooker with nonstick spray. Arrange apple slices over the bottom of the slow cooker.

2. Add the orange juice and water to a small bowl or measuring cup; stir to mix. Evenly drizzle over the apples.

3. In a small bowl, add the pecans, honey, coconut butter, and cinnamon, and mix well. Evenly crumble the pecan mixture over the apples.

4. Cover and cook on high for 2 hours or on low for 4 hours. Serve warm or chilled, as desired.

PER SERVING: Calories: 171 | Fat: 5g | Protein: 1g | Sodium: 1mg | Fiber: 3g | Carbohydrates: 34g | Sugar: 29g

Paleo "Butterscotch-Caramel" Glazed Nuts

These nuts taste even better when sprinkled over some Crustless Apple Pie (above).

INGREDIENTS | SERVES 32

4 cups raw almonds, pecan halves, or walnut halves

½ cup Paleo "Butterscotch-Caramel" Sauce (page 75)

1½ teaspoons cinnamon (optional)

1. Add all the ingredients to a 1-quart slow cooker. Stir to coat the nuts. Cover and cook on low for 3 hours, stirring at least once an hour.

2. Uncover and cook on low for 1 more hour, stirring every 20 minutes, until the nuts are almost dry.

3. Evenly spread the nuts on a lined baking sheet and let cool completely. Store in a covered container.

PER SERVING: Calories: 79 | Fat: 6g | Protein: 3g | Sodium: 0mg | Fiber: 2g | Carbohydrates: 5g | Sugar: 3g

Cinnamon-Spiced Apple Butter

If you're using a less tart apple, add the honey ¼ cup at a time until you reach desired sweetness. Serve over a slow-cooked dessert or breakfast dish.

INGREDIENTS | YIELDS 6 (½-CUP) SERVINGS

8 large or 12 medium Granny Smith apples

½ cup apple juice

¾ cup honey

2 teaspoons ground cinnamon

½ teaspoon allspice

½ teaspoon ground cloves

1. Wash, peel, core, and quarter the apples. Add to a 2-quart slow cooker along with the juice. Cover and cook on high for 4 hours.

2. Use an immersion blender to purée the apples. Stir in the honey, cinnamon, allspice, and cloves. Taste for seasoning and adjust if necessary.

3. Reduce the temperature of the slow cooker to low. Cook uncovered for 2 hours or until the apple butter is thick and dark. Store in the refrigerator for several weeks or freeze until needed.

PER SERVING: (½ cup) | Calories: 141 | Fat: 0g | Protein: 0g | Sodium: 3mg | Fiber: 1g | Carbohydrates: 38g | Sugar: 37g

Winter Warmer

Escape the bitter cold and warm up with this hot, comforting drink.

INGREDIENTS | SERVES 6

1 small cinnamon stick, broken into 1-inch pieces

¼ teaspoon ground cloves

¼ teaspoon nutmeg

¼ cup lemon juice

⅔ cup honey

1 bottle dry red wine

Thin lemon slices, for garnish

1. Combine all the ingredients except lemon slices in a 2-quart slow cooker.

2. Heat on high for 1 hour, or until hot, then reduce to low to hold temperature for serving.

3. Ladle into cocktail glasses and top each serving with a lemon slice.

PER SERVING: Calories: 217 | Fat: 0g | Protein: 0g | Sodium: 9mg | Fiber: 0g | Carbohydrates: 35g | Sugar: 32g

Orange Pudding Cake

Creamsicle and Orange Julius fans will love this dessert. It also works well with lemon juice and lemon zest instead of the orange. The beaten egg whites act as the leavening; the pudding forms on the bottom as the cake cooks.

INGREDIENTS | SERVES 6

4 large eggs, separated
⅓ cup fresh orange juice
1 tablespoon orange zest
3 tablespoons coconut butter, softened
1½ cups coconut milk
1 cup almond flour
1 cup honey
Nonstick cooking spray

1. Add the egg yolks, orange juice, orange zest, and coconut butter to a food processor; process for 30 seconds to cream the ingredients together. Continue to process while you slowly pour in the coconut milk.

2. In a medium bowl, combine the almond flour and honey. Stir to mix.

3. Pour the egg yolk mixture into the bowl and stir to combine it.

4. Add the egg whites to a separate chilled bowl; whip until stiff peaks form. Fold into the cake batter.

5. Pour into a greased (with nonstick spray) 2-quart or smaller slow cooker. Cover and cook on low for 2–2½ hours or until the cake is set on top.

PER SERVING: Calories: 445 | Fat: 25g | Protein: 10g | Sodium: 57mg | Fiber: 2g | Carbohydrates: 54g | Sugar: 49g

Lemon Pudding Pie

Try this recipe with a Paleo-approved "crumb" topping.

INGREDIENTS | SERVES 6

Nonstick cooking spray
¾ cup honey
¼ cup arrowroot powder
3 eggs, whisked
1 cup coconut milk
¼ cup lemon juice
1 teaspoon vanilla extract

1. Grease a 4-quart slow cooker with cooking spray.

2. In a small bowl, stir the honey and arrowroot powder together.

3. In a separate bowl, stir the eggs, coconut milk, lemon juice, and vanilla.

4. Combine the two mixtures and stir to form batter. Pour into slow cooker, cover, and cook on high for 2–4 hours, until the center has set and browned.

5. Let sit for 20 minutes before serving.

PER SERVING: Calories: 262 | Fat: 11g | Protein: 4g | Sodium: 44mg | Fiber: 0g | Carbohydrates: 42g | Sugar: 35g

Apple-Date "Crisp"

*Golden Delicious apples are suggested here, but go ahead
and try a different type of baking apple of your choice.*

INGREDIENTS | SERVES 6

6 cups peeled and thinly sliced Golden
Delicious apples

2 teaspoons lemon juice

⅓ cup chopped dates

1⅓ cups finely chopped almonds

½ cup almond flour

½ cup honey

½ teaspoon ground cinnamon

½ teaspoon ground ginger

Dash of ground nutmeg

Dash of ground cloves

4 tablespoons coconut butter

1. Combine apples, lemon juice, and dates in a bowl, and mix well. Transfer mixture to a 4½-quart slow cooker.

2. In a separate bowl, combine the almonds, flour, honey, cinnamon, ginger, nutmeg, and cloves. Cut in coconut butter with two knives or a pastry blender. Sprinkle nut mixture over apples and smooth down.

3. Cook on low for 4 hours. Serve warm.

PER SERVING: Calories: 290 | Fat: 15g | Protein: 7g | Sodium: 2mg | Fiber: 5g | Carbohydrates: 38g | Sugar: 31g

Paleo Crisp Variations

Experiment with a variety of Paleo-approved crisp ingredients like walnuts and pecans. Try using coconut or canola oil, or a combination of the two, instead of coconut butter.

Toasted Hazelnuts and Dates

Hazelnuts should be toasted on a baking sheet in a preheated 350°F oven for 8–10 minutes before using.

INGREDIENTS | SERVES 8

2 cups pitted dates, soaked in water overnight

⅔ cup boiling water

½ cup honey

Strips of peel from 1 lemon (yellow part only)

¼ cup hazelnuts, shelled and toasted

1. Drain the dates and place in a 4½-quart slow cooker.

2. Add boiling water, honey, and lemon peel. Cover and cook on high for 3 hours.

3. Discard lemon peel. Place dates in serving dishes and sprinkle with hazelnuts.

PER SERVING: Calories: 212 | Fat: 2g | Protein: 2g | Sodium: 2mg | Fiber: 4g | Carbohydrates: 51g | Sugar: 46g

Peach Cobbler

Cobbler is a versatile sweet dish that can be enjoyed as a warm and tasty eye opener or as a post-dinner dessert.

INGREDIENTS | SERVES 8

2 (16-ounce) packages frozen peaches, thawed and drained

¾ cup plus 1 tablespoon honey, divided

2 teaspoons ground cinnamon, divided

½ teaspoon ground nutmeg

¾ cup almond flour

6 tablespoons coconut butter

1. Combine the peaches, ¾ cup honey, 1½ teaspoons cinnamon, and nutmeg in a bowl. Transfer to a 4½-quart slow cooker.

2. In a separate bowl, combine the flour with remaining honey and cinnamon.

3. Cut in coconut butter with two knives or a pastry blender, and then spread mixture over peaches.

4. Cover and cook on high for 2 hours.

5. Serve warm.

PER SERVING: Calories: 211 | Fat: 6g | Protein: 3g | Sodium: 1mg | Fiber: 3g | Carbohydrates: 42g | Sugar: 38g

Appendix A

Paleo "Yes" and "No" Foods

In order to ensure your success on the Paleolithic diet, you need to stock your pantry with fresh, organic produce and grass-fed and barn-roaming meats. Feel free to experiment with items you would not normally choose. That will spice things up and keep you interested in the diet. Also listed here are the foods you should avoid, including processed grains, potatoes, legumes, and dairy.

Paleo "Yes" Foods

Protein

- Alligator
- Bass
- Bear
- Beef, lean and trimmed
- Bison
- Bluefish
- Caribou
- Chicken breast
- Chuck steak
- Clams
- Cod
- Crab
- Crayfish
- Egg whites
- Eggs
- Flank steak
- Game hen breasts
- Goat
- Grouper
- Haddock
- Halibut
- Hamburger, extra lean
- Herring
- Liver (beef, lamb, goat, or chicken)
- Lobster
- London broil
- Mackerel
- Marrow (beef, lamb, or goat)
- Mussels
- Orange roughy
- Ostrich
- Oysters
- Pheasant
- Pork chops
- Pork loin
- Pork, lean
- Quail
- Rabbit
- Rattlesnake
- Red snapper
- Salmon, wild-caught
- Scallops
- Scrod
- Shrimp
- Tilapia
- Tongue (beef, lamb, or goat)
- Trout
- Tuna, canned, unsalted
- Tuna, fresh
- Turkey breast
- Veal, lean
- Venison

Leafy Vegetables

- Arugula
- Beet greens
- Bitterleaf
- Bok choy
- Broccoli rabe
- Brussels sprouts
- Cabbage
- Celery
- Chard
- Chicory
- Chinese cabbage
- Collard greens
- Dandelion

- Endive
- Fiddlehead
- Kale
- Lettuce
- Radicchio
- Spinach
- Swiss chard
- Turnip
- Watercress
- Yarrow

Fruiting Vegetables

- Avocado
- Bell pepper
- Cucumber
- Eggplant
- Squash
- Sweet pepper
- Tomatillo
- Tomato
- Zucchini

Flowers and Flower Buds

- Artichoke
- Broccoli
- Cauliflower

Bulb and Stem Vegetables

- Asparagus
- Celery
- Florence fennel
- Garlic
- Kohlrabi
- Leek
- Onion

Sea Vegetables and Herbs of All Types

Fruits

- Apple
- Apricot
- Banana
- Blackberries
- Blueberries
- Cantaloupe
- Cherries
- Coconut
- Cranberries (not dried)
- Figs
- Grapefruit
- Grapes
- Guava
- Honeydew melon
- Kiwi
- Lemon
- Lime
- Mandarin orange
- Mango
- Nectarine
- Orange
- Papaya
- Passion fruit
- Peaches
- Pears
- Persimmon
- Pineapple
- Plums
- Pomegranate
- Raspberries
- Rhubarb
- Star fruit

- Strawberries
- Tangerine
- Watermelon
- All other fruits are acceptable

Fats, Nuts, Seeds, Oils, and Fatty Proteins

- Almond butter
- Almonds
- Avocado
- Brazil nuts
- Canola oil
- Cashew
- Cashew butter
- Chestnuts
- Coconut oil
- Flaxseed oil
- Hazelnuts/filberts
- Macadamia butter
- Macadamia nuts
- Olive oil
- Pecans
- Pine nuts
- Pistachios
- Pumpkin seeds
- Safflower oil
- Sesame seeds
- Sunflower butter, unsweetened
- Sunflower seeds
- Udo's oil
- Walnut oil
- Walnuts

Paleo "No" Foods

Legume Vegetables

- American groundnut
- Azuki beans
- Black-eyed peas
- Chickpeas (garbanzo bean)
- Common beans
- Fava beans
- Green beans
- Guar
- Indian peas
- Kidney beans
- Lentils
- Lima beans
- Mung beans
- Navy beans
- Okra
- Peanut
- Peanut butter
- Peas
- Pigeon peas
- Pinto beans
- Red beans
- Rice beans
- Snow peas
- Soybean and soy products
- String beans
- Sugar snap peas
- White beans

Dairy Foods

- All processed foods made with any dairy products
- Butter

- Cheese
- Cream
- Dairy spreads
- Frozen yogurt
- Ice cream
- Ice milk
- Low-fat milk
- Nonfat dairy creamer
- Powdered milk
- Skim milk
- Whole milk
- Yogurt

Cereal Grains

- Barley
- Corn
- Millet
- Oats
- Rice
- Rye
- Sorghum
- Wheat
- Wild rice

Cereal Grain-Like Seeds

- Amaranth
- Buckwheat
- Quinoa

Starchy Vegetables

- Starchy tubers
- Cassava root
- Manioc
- Potatoes and all potato products

- Sweet potatoes or yams (unless after workout to replenish glycogen)
- Tapioca pudding

Salt-Containing Foods, Fatty Meats, and Sugar

- Almost all commercial salad dressings and condiments
- Bacon
- Beef ribs
- Candy
- Canned salted meat or fish
- Chicken and turkey legs, thighs, and wings
- Chicken and turkey skin
- Deli meats
- Fatty ground beef
- Fatty pork cuts
- Frankfurters
- Ham
- Ketchup
- Lamb roast
- Olives
- Pickled foods
- Pork rinds
- Processed meats
- Salami
- Salt
- Salted nuts
- Salted spices
- Sausages
- Smoked, dried, and salted fish and meat
- Soft drinks and fruit juice
- Sugar

Appendix B

Paleo Athlete Modifications

Pre-Exercise Fuel: At least two hours before exercise or competition

Goals
- Consume low fiber and low glycemic index carbohydrates
- Include protein
- Hydrate

Examples: fruit (lower in fiber), i.e. applesauce, homemade smoothies (with fruit, small amount of fruit juice, and a few tablespoons of protein powder), sports bars (low in fiber and fat)

During Exercise Fuel:
Per hour of exercise

Goals
- Consume higher glycemic index carbohydrates, approximately 60 grams per hour
- Prevent dehydration

Examples: Sports drinks are best during training and competition, especially in hot and humid climates.

Post-Exercise Fuel: Within thirty minutes, and until ninety minutes after

Goals
- Replace carbohydrate stores (a.k.a. muscle glycogen)
- Promote muscle repair and recover (protein)
- Rehydrate (fluid and electrolytes)

Examples: liquid carbohydrates (i.e. sports drinks with protein); protein drink/homemade smoothies; non-Paleo foods are encouraged here (sports drinks, jelly, fruit juices, starchy vegetables) along with lean proteins (chicken, turkey, tuna, etc.)

Adapted from *The Paleo Diet for Athletes*. © 2005. Loren Cordain, PhD, and Joe Friel, MS.

Appendix C

Paleo Substitutions

INGREDIENT	PALEO SUBSTITUTIONS
cow's milk	coconut, almond, macadamia, or hazelnut milk
bacon	uncured bacon and meats
deli meat	fresh-cut chicken or turkey breast, thinly sliced
salad dressing	oil and lemon or lime juice
vinegar	lemon or lime juice
starch	spaghetti squash, butternut squash, acorn squash
sugar	raw honey
soda	fruit-infused water, iced tea
salt	lemon juice, spices, fresh herbs
butter	nut oils, coconut butter
peanut butter	all other nut and seed butters
cookies	fresh fruit
chocolate	cacao
commercially prepared meat	grass-fed, barn-roaming meat
farm-raised fish	wild-caught fish
baked desserts	baked fruit
wheat flour	almond flour
breadcrumbs	arrowroot powder
cream	full-fat coconut milk or coconut butter

Standard U.S./Metric Measurement Conversions

VOLUME CONVERSIONS

U.S. Volume Measure	Metric Equivalent
⅛ teaspoon	0.5 milliliters
¼ teaspoon	1 milliliters
½ teaspoon	2 milliliters
1 teaspoon	5 milliliters
½ tablespoon	7 milliliters
1 tablespoon (3 teaspoons)	15 milliliters
2 tablespoons (1 fluid ounce)	30 milliliters
¼ cup (4 tablespoons)	60 milliliters
⅓ cup	90 milliliters
½ cup (4 fluid ounces)	125 milliliters
⅔ cup	160 milliliters
¾ cup (6 fluid ounces)	180 milliliters
1 cup (16 tablespoons)	250 milliliters
1 pint (2 cups)	500 milliliters
1 quart (4 cups)	1 liter (about)

WEIGHT CONVERSIONS

U.S. Weight Measure	Metric Equivalent
½ ounce	15 grams
1 ounce	30 grams
2 ounces	60 grams
3 ounces	85 grams
¼ pound (4 ounces)	115 grams
½ pound (8 ounces)	225 grams
¾ pound (12 ounces)	340 grams
1 pound (16 ounces)	454 grams

OVEN TEMPERATURE CONVERSIONS

Degrees Fahrenheit	Degrees Celsius
200 degrees F	95 degrees C
250 degrees F	120 degrees C
275 degrees F	135 degrees C
300 degrees F	150 degrees C
325 degrees F	160 degrees C
350 degrees F	180 degrees C
375 degrees F	190 degrees C
400 degrees F	205 degrees C
425 degrees F	220 degrees C
450 degrees F	230 degrees C

BAKING PAN SIZES

American	Metric
8 × 1½ inch round baking pan	20 × 4 cm cake tin
9 × 1½ inch round baking pan	23 × 3.5 cm cake tin
1 × 7 × 1½ inch baking pan	28 × 18 × 4 cm baking tin
13 × 9 × 2 inch baking pan	30 × 20 × 5 cm baking tin
2 quart rectangular baking dish	30 × 20 × 3 cm baking tin
15 × 10 × 2 inch baking pan	30 × 25 × 2 cm baking tin (Swiss roll tin)
9 inch pie plate	22 × 4 or 23 × 4 cm pie plate
7 or 8 inch springform pan	18 or 20 cm springform or loose bottom cake tin
9 × 5 × 3 inch loaf pan	23 × 13 × 7 cm or 2 lb narrow loaf or pate tin
1½ quart casserole	1.5 litre casserole
2 quart casserole	2 litre casserole

Index

Note: Page numbers in **bold** indicate recipe category lists.